THE POETIC THEMES OF ROBERT LOWELL

JEROME MAZZARO

∧

The
Poetic Themes
of
Robert Lowell

Ann Arbor
The University of Michigan Press

For Ray, Pat, and Randy Malbone

Acknowledgments

I would like to thank the John Simon Guggenheim Memorial Foundation for a fellowship, part of which was diverted to complete this manuscript. Also, as a book of this kind is seldom the work of one man, despite what title pages read, I should like to thank people whose encouragements, information, and criticism have contributed to its completion. They are David Herreshoff, David Hettich, C. Carroll Hollis, Chester Jorgenson, Robert Peckham, Dale Renguette, T. J. Ross, and W. D. Snodgrass. I should also like to thank the following people, magazines, and publishers for kind permission to quote copyrighted material:

Robert Lowell, *The Kenyon Review*, and The Cummington Press for "The Cities' Summer Death," copyright 1939, by *The Kenyon Review*, and *Land of Unlikeness*, copyright 1944, by Robert Lowell.

Harcourt, Brace & World, Inc. for "The Exile's Return," "Mary Winslow," "At the Indian Killer's Grave," "The Quaker Graveyard in Nantucket," "In Memory of Arthur Winslow," "To Peter Taylor on the Feast of the Epiphany," "The Dead in Europe," "As a Plane Tree by the Water," "The North Sea Undertaker's Complaint," "Buttercups," "Mr. Edwards and the Spider," "The Death of the Sheriff," "Her Dead Brother," and "Where the Rainbow Ends." From *Lord Weary's Castle*, by Robert Lowell, copyright 1944, 1946, by Robert Lowell. And for "The Mills of the Kavanaughs," "Falling Asleep over the Aeneid," "Between the Porch and the Altar," "Mother Marie

Contents

CHAPTER ONE
Beginnings

In 1944 a slim volume of poetry, *Land of Unlikeness*, appeared, bringing the work of Robert Lowell to the attention of American book buyers. In the Introduction to the volume, Allen Tate described its author as "consciously a Catholic poet," whose "style is bold and powerful" and whose "symbolic language often has the effect of being *willed*." The poetry, readers were told, "points to the disappearance of the Christian experience from the modern world, and stands, perhaps, for the poet's own effort to recover it." But, Tate warned, "the spiritual decay is not universal, ... there is at least a memory of the spiritual dignity of man, now sacrificed to mere secularization and a craving for mechanical order."

For readers of "little magazines," Robert Lowell and his message needed little introduction. Since 1939 his work had appeared in the pages of *The Chimera*, *The Kenyon*, *The Partisan*, and *The Sewanee* reviews. However, Tate's Introduction does suggest that before a reader can do justice to Robert Lowell's poetry the particular view he holds as poet and Catholic should be defined. This view, for the most part, derives from such sources as James Joyce, Gerard Manley Hopkins, T. S. Eliot, St. Ignatius, Dante, and St. Bernard of Clairvaux. It conceives of the poet as a synthesizer of thought and of the literary imagination in terms closely akin to religious meditation. As an aesthetic theory, it is perhaps most clearly pursued in William F. Lynch's *Christ and Apollo* (Mentor-Omega Books, 1963): "There will come a place in these explorations when

1

we will want to look into the formal question of whether there is a theological level at the innermost core of the literary image." At that "place," Father Lynch establishes that there is such a level and proposes "the *Spiritual Exercises* of St. Ignatius as a source of poetic as well as spiritual insight ..., where we are concluding our first investigations into the image of the definite and the image of time, for he has much to say about both." It should be added that meditation, "the application of the mind and will to some spiritual principle, mystery, or event, for the purpose of sanctifying one's soul by exciting proper spiritual emotions and resolving on a course of action," differs from contemplation, "an imperfect vision of the Supreme Being and of His infinite perfections." The two terms must be kept separate although, like St. Ignatius, Lowell sometimes merges the purposes of both.

As Lowell derives his ideas and terms of art from Joyce and others, it might be well to review their terminologies. In the closing chapter of *The Portrait of the Artist as a Young Man,* Joyce defines three basic positions of aesthetic involvement and explains their effects on literature. These positions of involvement are lyrical, epical, and dramatic, and an explanation of each does much to illuminate Lowell's aesthetic positions in *Land of Unlikeness* as well as to suggest the future direction of his work. The lyrical form, "the simplest verbal vesture of an instant emotion," concerns itself more with the emotion than with the poet's feeling the emotion. As William Wordsworth expressed the idea in his "Preface to the *Lyrical Ballads,*" it is the "spontaneous overflow of powerful emotion." This emotion without a clearly defined "persona," according to Joyce, manifests itself in what might be loosely termed "personal" and "mood" poetry.

Joyce sees the epical form as emerging out of the lyrical form and as distinguished from it by the artist's prolonged brooding "upon himself as centre of an epical event ... till the centre of emotional gravity is equidistant from the artist himself and from others." This form contains two complications above those of the lyrical form, for, in addition to emotion, the artist must have an "epical event," an event comparable to that described by the psychologist Carl Jung as a primordial image or archetype. Like the episode in the epic poem, this event must be important to the history of a nation or a race. Further, to express his emotions, the poet needs to develop a "persona," or voice, which is as well drawn and objective as any of the other personages of his poem. This "persona" is usually the poet objectified by the rigors of an intense self-examination, the man as he knows himself to be. The result is "mythic literature," which T. S. Eliot calls "the most important expression which the present age has found." "In using the myth," Eliot comments on *Ulysses*, "in manipulating a continuous parallel between contemporaneity and antiquity, Mr. Joyce is pursuing a method which others must pursue after him. They will not be imitators, any more than the scientist who uses the discoveries of an Einstein in pursuing his own, independent, further investigations. It is simply a way of controlling, of ordering, of giving shape and a significance to the immense panorama of futility and anarchy which is contemporary history."

The dramatic form is reached, Joyce states, when the vitality with which the poet has saturated his personages "fills every person with such vital force that he or she assumes a proper and intangible esthetic life." In short, the dramatic form occurs when the characters of a poem take on an identity independent of the poet, and the poem becomes an expression of this identity or an interplay of the expression of several of these identities. As such, in theological terms, it is the highest form of aesthetic distance, for it most nearly approximates the loss of egoism necessary for the rapt awareness of God in the contemplative experience.

These distinctions follow closely equally important distinctions which are made in descriptions of Christian meditational exercises derived from St. Ignatius' *Spiritual Exercises*. Lowell gets them from John Pick's *Hopkins, Priest and Poet* (London, 1942). However, by the time Lowell uses them in his poems, he has gone by way of Dante past Pick to the original sources in St. Bernard and St. Bonaventure. The first of these exercises—imagining oneself present at the very spot where the event occurred—corresponds closely to the "mood" or lyrical form of Joyce. The second and third—imagining the events as occurring before one's very eyes, and imagining everything so that it assumes a life of its own—likewise correspond to the epical and dramatic forms of Joyce and may well have been their source.

The connection of these exercises with literature is stressed by both Pick and Father Lynch. "It is almost impossible to exaggerate the importance of the Spiritual Exercises in the life of a Jesuit," Pick notes. "His [Hopkins'] attitude toward poetry and fame was shaped by them." Less specifically concerned, Father Lynch demonstrates that as St. Ignatius was completely human, time-possessed, and definite in the method of the exercises, the emphasis on concreteness contributes to the literary imagination, but as the method assumes the ultimate objective to be contemplative love, it becomes destructive to art, an "escape-theology." This conflict between concretely sensuous and ecstatic perceptions is the same conflict faced by Dante throughout his *Paradiso*. As Eliot wrote, "Dante has to educate our senses as he goes along." Pick related the problem more specifically: "The difficulty of the artist and the religious takes an enigmatic form; the sensuous beauty of the world attracts the artist: Hopkins' undergraduate note-books are filled with notations of one keenly sensitive to natural beauty, of one anxious to translate into words his awareness of shape, texture, colour; on the other hand, his religious asceticism makes him reject the senses. And the deficiencies of his undergraduate poetry, both secular and religious, may largely be told in terms of the conflict." It is a conflict which Lowell, likewise, will have to face.

In any case, a knowledge of both sets of distinctions becomes essential for an understanding of Lowell's position as poet and Catholic, for the ideas of art and aesthetic distance they instill strongly affect the style and content of art. The distinctions lead not so much to an exclusion of subject matter from poetry as to a special manner of including what the poet wishes to include. Since Lowell had embraced the substance of these distinctions long before the publication of *Land of Unlikeness*, it might prove useful, before discussing the particular views of the book, to retrace his steps as they led to his acceptance of this highly religious and formal style and point of view. These steps begin with the publication of the first version of "Death from Cancer" as an undergraduate poem written at Kenyon College. This version, "The Cities' Summer Death," written in four four-line stanzas, describes the death in March 1938 of Lowell's grandfather Arthur Winslow, a retired mining executive. It appeared in the September 1939 issue of *The Kenyon Review* and differs greatly from the more widely known version in Part One of the four-part "In Memory of Arthur Winslow":

> *The summer hospital enframes*
> *In its fashionable windows*

Beginnings

Boats brow-beaten by varnished storms
And curbed-off grass where no cows browse.

Grandfather feathery as thought
Furls his flurried wrapper and floats
Off his adjustable bed
Wafted on somnolent swan-boats.

Cancer ossifies his features,
The starved skeleton shows its teeth,
Flamingo crackling embroiders
Italian bones with shameless froth.

But the honking untainted swans
Float over the deathly stream
And the aghast oarsmen of Charon's
Ferry raise their skeleton rhythm.

In Joycean terms, the poem is "lyrical." It does not combine its description and emotive language into the distinctive persona required of epical verse. But even as a lyrical poem it fails. Stylistically it lacks distinction and contains little, if any, of the vitality and close texture which characterizes lyrical verse of this time. In their place, Lowell substitutes obscurity, and this causes him to fail in what is a first principle of writing—communication—for it places a barrier of unconveyed information between the event, the poet, and the reader.

Part of the obscurity is a by-product of Lowell's attempt to generalize and universalize physical detail. His picture of the hospital in which Winslow dies as "windows" and the park as "curbed-off grass" destroys immediacy and a sense of locale. But most of the obscurity is the result of his referents' having remained too personal and the situation's having become too mysterious to be grasped fully. This is particularly noticeable in the image of the "flamingo crackling" of the skeleton's teeth. But it also exists in Lowell's selection of words and in his techniques. Why, one might ask, is the grandfather's wrapper "flurried" and why are the swan-boats "somnolent"? The first suggests haste, the second slowness. Likewise, why does Lowell use "And curbed-off grass where no cows browse" for public gardens and then crowd lines like "Flamingo crackling embroiders / Italian bones with shameless froth"? One might ask, too, why the swans are "untainted," or wonder when he reads "summer hospital," "varnished storms," "flurried wrapper" and "somnolent swan-boats" if Lowell may not have overdone the classical device of dislocated modifiers.

Nevertheless, despite its failure, the poem does adumbrate some important techniques. In the opening lines, with "enframes" and "windows," there is a hint at the word interplay which critics such as I. A. Richards feel is essential to good poetry and which becomes more common in Lowell's later work. Moreover, in light of the other pat images of the poem, the grandfather's turning into a skeleton presents a surprisingly effective image. And with the final images of the poem, the honking of the swans before death and the implied association of the Charles River and the Acheron, the classical allusions which frequent Lowell's work appear. The images suggest the subsequent epical and multilevel presentations which continue in Lowell's writing.

The revision of the poem which appeared in *The Sewanee Review* (1943) illustrates Lowell's development as a poet during the four-year interval and emphasizes in part the effects of a course in Dante and of his conversion three years earlier to Roman Catholicism. The new version, "Death from Cancer on Easter," reads:

This Easter, Arthur Winslow, less than dead
Your people set you up in Phillips House
To settle off your wrangle with the crab
Whose claws drop flesh on your serge yachting blouse,
Until longshoreman Charon come and stab
Through your Procrustes' bed,
And catch the crab. On Boston Basin, shells
Hit water by the Union Boat Club's wharf;
You ponder why the coxes' squeakings dwarf
The resurrexit Dominus of all the bells;

Grandfather Winslow, look, the swanboats coast
That island in the Public Gardens, where
The bread-stuffed ducks are brooding, where with tub
And strainer the mid-Sunday Irish scare
The sun-struck shallows for the dusky chub,
This Easter, and the Ghost
With seven wounds walks on the waves to bear

Beginnings

Arthur upon a trumpeting black swan
Beyond Charles River to the Acheron
Where timbers draw no water for the voyager.

Now in ten-line stanzas reminiscent of Matthew Arnold's "Thyrsis," the ideas of the poem are clearer, although the poem is more packed with personal, classical, and religious allusions. Phillips House, Boston Basin, Union Boat Club, and Public Gardens set the poem unmistakably in Boston. The crab image of lines 3 and 7 clears when one realizes that the astrological sign of Cancer is a crab, and the interplay on it—"where claws drop flesh" and "longshoreman Charon"—suggests that an added meaning, that of a dock machine used to hoist and load cargo, is intended in line 3. Charon moves up significantly from the last stanza to the first to oppose a new figure, Christ, introduced in the second stanza as "the Ghost with seven wounds." The seven wounds echo the seven deadly sins of Dante's *Purgatorio* rather than the traditional five wounds of Christ. "Procrustes' bed" replaces the "adjustable bed" of the earlier version to suggest the possibility of the grandfather's adjusting by surgery to suit the bed rather than the bed's adjusting by machinery to suit Winslow. The name Procrustes suggests, too, the mutilation of the body which accompanies some types of cancer operations. "Serge yachting blouse," "shells," "coxes" (coxswain) reflect Winslow's—and consequently Lowell's—Back Bay heritage. The *resurrexit Dominus* adds a note of triumphal irony which becomes typical of Lowell and his choice of scenes: a man dying while the bells proclaim the resurrection of Christ from the dead with the theological implications of the ultimate resurrection of all the dead. The successful interplay here of personal and traditional levels reveals some of the power of Lowell's early techniques at their best. The bells also suggest the offices being sung by those souls in Purgatory awaiting their purification.

As the situation of the poem has not altered, the swanboats return in the second stanza, for Phillip's House—situated near the Public Garden—leaves both versions open to the particular image. "Bread-stuffed ducks" in line 13 is one of several realistic observations which fill the stanza; the ducks have been overfed by people in the park. The Irish, in another such observation, are fishing for chub in the shallows of the Garden's pond. Both prepare the reader for the acceptance of the more symbolic images which close the poem and suggest, additionally, the miraculous multiplication of bread and fish which occurs in the Bible immediately before Christ walks on the waters. With "trumpeting black swan," Lowell reinserts the classical idea that a swan utters a cry before death, and here, with "trumpeting" rather than "honking," he further suggests that Winslow would be welcomed in heaven.

The image of the black swan accentuates this idea when one becomes aware of Lowell's invectives against laissez-faire capitalism in "Concord," Winslow's industrial position, and Sir Walter Raleigh's proverbial variation on Juvenal's *nigroque simillima cygno:* "Only those few black Swans I must except, who having had the grace to value worldly vanities at no more than their own price; do, by retaining the comfortable memory of a well-acted life, behold Death without dread. . . ." At least the reader can now safely assume that in the first version it is Winslow and not the swan who is "untainted," although the quality may be intended ultimately for both. In conjunction with death, the swan also invites a favorable comparison of the qualities of King Arthur with those of Arthur Winslow, whose journey to afterlife resembles that monarch's epic swan journey to Avalon.

Finally, a direct rather than implied comparison is made between the Charles River and the Acheron, the waters of life flowing into the waters of death. The last line, "Where timbers draw no water for the voyager," indicates that Winslow dead has no body weight, so that the boat does not sink deeper into the river. This echoes the lines in Canto II of the *Purgatorio* where Dante meets "con un vasello snelletto e leggiero, / tanto che l'acqua nulla ne inghiottiva" ("with a vessel so swift and light that the waters nowise drew it in") and opposes Aeneas' crossing in Book VI of the *Aeneid:* "gemuit sub pondere cumba / subtilis et multam accepit rimosa paludem" ("The patched boat groaned under the weight, and full of cracks receives much [water from the] lake").

The most immediate stylistic change seems to be in the language of the poem. The language shifts from a presentation of generalized detail to a presentation of specific detail and introduces with this second version a new Christian imagery. The image of Christ coming to fetch the dead replaces the traditional one of Charon. "Longshoreman Charon," whose job seems to be merely to load the boats in port, stands opposed to the "wave-walking" Christ, who comes half-way over the water to meet the faithful, and is far different from the Vergilian ferryman of the earlier ver-

8

sion. The result is a strange new mixture of pagan and Christian doctrine: The faithful called over the Acheron succeed in crossing the water to heaven only while they, like Peter in the water-walking episode in the Bible, have faith in Christ. Those who doubt sink into the river where, one may assume, they clamor *ad infinitum,* like the souls in the *Aeneid* who are not permitted to get into the boat because they have not been duly buried.

Another evident change in the poem is that of tone. The purely descriptive and ornamental first version has taken on the qualities of a monologue. This monologue suggests the creation of an objective persona, or speaker, for rather than artificially poetic, the diction is modified to fit everyday speech patterns. Thus, along with the emergence of an epical event—Winslow's journey to afterlife—an epical persona emerges, and a relationship between Winslow and this persona is established. Reflected mainly in the poem's connotative use of language, this relationship contrasts greatly with the overtly confused language of the earlier version.

In the second stanza the language of the persona shifts slightly and takes on the tonal qualities of an Old Testament vision, Joel's vision, for example, of the Last Judgment, or Ezekiel's vision of the destruction of Jerusalem. As a result the whole seemingly confused journey of the soul in the second version contrasts greatly and favorably with the pat and literary ferryride of "The Cities' Summer Death," and indicates Lowell's concern with salvation may be genuine, not borrowed cleverly like his images from the underworlds of previous poets.

Perhaps the most significant change in the poem is that it has begun to borrow devices from the meditative tradition. Gone is the attempt to achieve "universality" by blurring the individual into the species. Like the religious meditator, the poet has begun to compose his visions as vividly as possible, so that he may place both himself and his reader in the place where the event occurred, so that he may, in turn, recover these events or, more significantly, achieve the eventual religious colloquies of a contemplative encounter. He can proceed in such a direction because, like the meditator, he believes that he can enter as fully as possible into the entire concreteness of every distinct moment of "Christological" time.

The third and last version of the poem to be considered here in detail is the one which appeared in *Land of Unlikeness.* This version, very little different from the one previously quoted, is, except for the deletion of "serge" in line 4 and changes in punctuation, the same as the one which appeared in *Lord Weary's Castle* (1946). Along with word changes in the first stanza, the important differences of this new version occur mainly in the second stanza.

In line 3 of the first stanza "wrangle" is replaced by "wrestling," which suggests a physical rather than a vocal struggle with the crab and fits the meaning and the sound of the line far better than the harsh and less precise "wrangle." In line 6 "Procrustes" is replaced by "adjusted," probably to heighten and clarify the opposition of Charon and Christ: Christ is being opposed to Charon, not to Charon and Procrustes. In the second stanza, "the Ghost with seven wounds" is replaced by "the Ghost of risen Jesus." Again, like the earlier replacing of "curbed-off grass" with "Public Garden," it is a removal of an implicit statement for a more explicit one. Finally, the last line of the poem is revised from "Where timbers draw no water for the voyager" to "Where the wide waters and their voyager are one." This change is not a change in meaning so much as an elimination of any confusion in the crossing of the Acheron: The reflective quality of water has made it a traditional Christian symbol for souls, and by its association with baptism water suggests purification. Unlike the earlier version, the crossing need no longer be made in a boat.

Essentially, what has been evolving throughout the versions of this poem is Lowell's peculiar style and point of view, characterized by his gradual development away from detachment to attachment, from exclusion to inclusion. No longer are his lines filled with the bland descriptions of his early poem. The surroundings affect the viewer and their effects are now put into verse. The events of today echo both those of yesterday and those of tomorrow and, like the chord struck on an organ, reverberate a fullness of being. As a result, the casual allusions in "The Cities' Summer Death" combine with the poet's present cultural and religiously directed allusions.

This fullness and the return to the meditational influences of the metaphysical poets, one critic, John Frederick Nims, terms an "inverse baroque." In this "baroque," the earlier loose lines are superceded by emotionally full lines. Boyish imitation gives way to maturer invention, creation, and occasionally overwriting. This overwriting is most manifest in the often melodramatic, nightmarish, and exaggerated situations which the poet uses to approximate his epical actions. In "Death from Cancer," it is evident in the way Arthur Winslow is made into a superhuman Arthurian figure. Lowell cannot present him simply as a human being.

Despite these changes, certain technical and thematic devices have remained constant in each of the revisions and are equally worth noting. The use of a single word, like "crab," to mean several things in the context of a poem is repeated in other Lowell poems. "Noli Me Tangere," for instance, in *Lord Weary's Castle* uses "wain" for both wagon and constellation, to bind up the images of the poem. The view of history which interplays the personal and the traditional and which is first dealt with here continues beyond these revisions to become a major force in *Land of Unlikeness*. The theme of suffering souls recurs in later poems, as in "The Dead in Europe." The Winslows return in "At the Indian Killer's Grave," "Buttercups," "The Quaker Graveyard in Nantucket," "Mary Winslow," and in many of the poems comprising Part IV of *Life Studies* (1959). Boston and New England form the background for much of Lowell's other poetry.

The other three sections of "In Memory of Arthur Winslow," appearing for the first time in *Land of Unlikeness*, offer themselves as extensions of "Death from Cancer," but on closer observation, really strike out in all the other major directions of Lowell's verse. As such, they provide an excellent place to conclude an introduction to Lowell's poetry. "Dunbarton," the second poem of the cycle (not to be confused with "Dunbarton" in *Life Studies*), brings the poet and the reader to the Winslow burial plot at Dunbarton and to the town which Arthur Winslow's progenitor, General John Stark, founded in New Hampshire 170 years earlier. The other two form disparate, later homages.

Thematically, "Dunbarton" begins as the first poem ends, with the burial of Winslow after his death from cancer. This burial is contrasted in the poem with the epic event of the founding of Plymouth Colony:

The stones are yellow and the grass is grey
When we ride you to the Dunbarton Hill
In a mortician's Packard limousine;
The dozen Winslows and the Starks half fill
The granite plot and the dwarfed pines go green
From watching for the day
When the great year of the little yoeman [sic] *come*

Bringing the Mayflower Compact and the faith
That made the Pilgrim Makers take a lathe
To point their wooden steeples lest the Word be dumb.

O fearful Witnesses, your day is done:
The minister, Kingsolving, waves your ghosts
To the shades, evergreen, the pilgrims' home;
The first selectman of Dunbarton posts
Wreathes of New Hampshire pine-cones on your chrome
Box where the mirrored sun
Is booming: "Arthur, no one living has reached
Dunbarton. Are only poor relations left
To hold an empty bag of pine-cones?" Cleft,
Broken down boulders sprawl out where our fathers preached.

The warm, "yellow" stones and the dead, "grey" grass form the major symbols of the contrast and become increasingly important to the reader as he proceeds to the rest of the poem. This dichotomy of life and death is the principal theme of this section, and color contributes most of what additional meaning he finds.

The rest of the first stanza is simple and direct description, outlining the drive to Dunbarton Hill in the mortician's Packard, where the mourners see the half-filled burial plot of Winslows and Starks. The lines in this respect are much like the opening ones of the second stanza of "Death from Cancer," a preparation for the more symbolic passages to follow. This is seen especially in the image of the "dwarfed pines" which "go green" with envy for the time when political and moral conviction will return to man. In the image Lowell realizes a new variation on the traditional with a scenic rather than a mythological continuity, the continuity of the persistence of natural landscape against the transience of human existence. The pines are the same as those which saw the "little yeoman come," bringing the Mayflower Compact. They are now dwarfed by the "we" of the poem, as the *resurrexit Dominus* of "Death from Cancer" had been dwarfed by the "coxes' squeakings" from the Union Boat Club wharf.

In the second stanza, Lowell addresses his ancestors—"O fearful Witnesses"—hovering there in spirit as the minister casts Winslow's symbolic dust to the winds, or in this case, to the "shades" and "pilgrims' home" of line 13. By altering the name of the minister who performed the ceremony from the Reverend Arthur Lee

Kinsolving to "Kingsolving" (King-dissolving) Lowell suggests the religious decay of the modern world and reveals part of the occasional vindictiveness of his uncompromising vision. As Basil Willey points out regarding Jonathan Swift in *Eighteenth Century Background* (New York, 1946), it is not always the function of the social critic to understand, for to do so may render tolerable the practices which he seeks to correct; to understand everything is too often to pardon it.

The suggested decay of religious values continues to the last line of the poem, which relies upon the "rock-faith" symbol of the Christian Church for its effect: "Cleft, / Broken down boulders sprawl out where our fathers preached." This theme is repeated in Lowell's "Where the Rainbow Ends," as well as in the sonnet, "Concord": "This Church is Concord, where the Emersons / Washed out the blood-clots on my Master's robe." Christ the King has been dissolved as Savior by the corruption of the world.

Also in the stanza, with the burial of Winslow, the minister puts away Winslow's interests, "his ghosts," to the "shades" and the "pilgrims' home," perhaps the blockhouse built at Marshfield by Edward Winslow, governor of Plymouth. The realistic world returns with a notation of the presence of a selectman of Dunbarton, honoring the dead Winslow with a wreath of New Hampshire pinecones, and the "sun," yellow and representing life, is described as offering the final tribute to Winslow—booming into the chrome of his coffin its twenty-one gun salute.

As "dwarfed" had earlier, the suggested shells of the sun's salute echo with "booming" the boat shells of "Death from Cancer," and indicate again the richness of meaning Lowell occasionally achieves in his selection of words. The message of the sun implies in still another way the decay of modern life. The Winslows have become "poor relations," poorer because they have lost "the faith / That made the Pilgrim Makers take a lathe / To point their wooden steeples."

In this poem which admittedly lessens the baroque complexity of the first, one notes the same stylistic interplay of the traditional and personal which marked the first part. Here, however, the traditional moves from a religious and literary to a more recognizable historical basis. Early Massachusetts and New Hampshire history, inextricably bound with the history of the Winslow family, is exploited, and if the poem seems more immediate it is mainly that an

American reader is more familiar with the background of the Pilgrims than he is with the theological and classical juxtapositions of "Death from Cancer." All the same, much of the poem's significance derives from this process of counterpointing, especially in what is being counterpointed. The stony coast of New Hampshire is set against the traditional symbolism of rocks to produce an effect, or else the observed color yellow, fused with the sun, is employed throughout the poem to give "life" reactions to surroundings. The pointed steeples, the Mayflower Compact, the pines, each similarly contributes its meaning to the poem and prepares the reader for the harshest section of the cycle.

This section, entitled "Five Years Later," is exactly what its title suggests, the personal recollection and disavowal of Winslow by Lowell five years after the mining executive's death:

> *This Easter, Arthur Winslow, five years gone,*
> *I come to bury you and not to praise*
> *The craft that netted a million dollars, late*
> *Mining in California's golden bays*
> *Then lost it all in Boston real estate;*
> *Then from the train, at dawn,*
> *Leaving Columbus in Ohio, shell*
> *On shell of our stark culture struck the sun*
> *To fill my head with all our fathers won*
> *When Cotton Mather wrestled with the fiends from Hell.*
>
> *You must have hankered for our family's craft:*
> *The block-house Edward made, the Governor,*
> *At Marshfield, and the slight coin-silver spoons*
> *Some Winslow hammered thinner than Revere,*
> *And General Stark's coarse bas-relief of bronze*
> *Set on your granite shaft*
> *In rough Dunbarton; for what else could bring*
> *You, Arthur, to the veined and alien West,*
> *But devil's notions that your gold, at least,*
> *Would give back life to men who whipped the British King?*

This disavowal is revealed in the numerous puns and borrowed ironies which fill the opening stanza. "Easter" and "burial" suggest the first irony, for Easter is a time of resurrection and new life, not of burial. The paraphrase of Shakespeare's *Julius Caesar*—with its obvious punning on "craft" (ability-vessel), its borrowing of cliché ("California's golden bays"), and its juxtapositions (mining-bays, California-Boston)—continues it. As Mark Antony's funeral oration was deliberately geared to stress the good in Caesar's life—that which is "oft interred with the bones," the reader is led by analogy to believe that for Winslow this "good" is not the humanity which Antony attributes to Caesar, but the materialistic pursuit of a million dollars. Thus, one sees again the severity with which Lowell sometimes deals with men. The severity is further heightened by the puns on "Columbus" and "stark" and that recurrent word "shell" which close the stanza.

The second stanza presents part of the ancestor worship which Lowell tries to end. His family is introduced: Edward Winslow (1595–1655), the governor of Plymouth 1633, 1636, and 1644, who came over on the "Mayflower" and built at Marshfield the blockhouse referred to in the poem; Edward Winslow (1669–1753), the governor's grandson and the second Winslow mentioned in the stanza, a high sheriff and silversmith, who was the son of Edward Winslow and Elizabeth Hutchinson Winslow; and General John Stark (1728–1822), a Revolutionary War general, who in 1759 devoted himself to the settlement of a new township, at first called Starkstown but later Dunbarton.

Each of these men achieved a reputation in American history. The first is cited by the *Dictionary of American Biography* for his contributions to government as "the first man to achieve success in England after receiving his training in affairs in America." The second, for his contributions to art, as having been able with his other accomplishments "to produce a quantity of fine silverwork, which for historical as well as esthetic reasons is among the silver most valued by American collectors." The last, for his successes as a general: "Oct. 4, 1777, he was promoted to the rank of brigadier-general in the Continental Service." Thus, Lowell has stressed the contributions to government, art, and war which Winslow's ancestors have made. These are weighed against his only accomplishment—the search for and discovery of gold in California. The attempt to achieve their stature and "give back life to men who whipped the British King" makes Winslow's life seem indeed small. It is quite a comedown from the settlers of a new Canaan and is recorded again in the closing lines of Lowell's poem, "Salem": "Where was it that New England bred the men / Who quartered the Leviathan's fat flanks / And fought the British lion to his knees?"

The interplay here of the closing lines of the opening stanza and the closing lines of the poem provides the substance of the poem. In the first stanza, Cotton Mather's wrestle with the fiends from Hell over the possession of men's souls is interpreted by Lowell as a wrestle with materialism which, in turn, Arthur Winslow with his "devil's notions of gold" pursues in order to give back to the ancestral line the stature of its tradition. In this respect, the action is much like the action of "Dunbarton," which can be reduced ultimately to the interaction of the "Puritan Makers" with that of the modern world.

Moreover, the picture here of Winslow differs greatly from that being whose soul floated down the Charles River to the Acheron in "Death from Cancer." Why, one wonders, is there this change in attitude? First, in this section of the cycle the emphasis shifts from what the man was to what the man stood for. Time perhaps accomplished this. But two other significant things happened in the five-year interval between Winslow's death and "Five Years Later" which might have led Lowell to his reevaluation: the outbreak of World War II and an ingraining of his Roman Catholicism.

Like Ezra Pound, Lowell found the war to be a product of moneyed interests rather than of principle, and he attacked it in several poems. In attacking the war and the money group ultimately responsible for it, Lowell was committed to a position which called for the reevaluation of Winslow, who allied himself with moneyed interests. And the effect of Lowell's Catholicism was to make him feel that Protestantism was allied with the capitalistic system which had propagated the war. Disillusionment, brought on by his attitude toward materialism and religious decay, is what Lowell chooses for the subject of the last part of the cycle.

In this section, "A Prayer for My Grandfather to Our Lady," he tries to redeem himself from any of the vindictiveness and near blasphemies of the earlier sections and sums up the totality of not only his relationship with tradition but also his relationship with contemporary existence. In form it is a colloquy with Our Lady. This kind of colloquy is a typical induction into a kind of contemplative experience stressed by St. Ignatius as the ultimate aim of the Spiritual Exercises. As such, it reflects on the earlier sections as religious meditations.

"Mother, for these three hundred years or more
Neither our clippers nor our slavers reached
The haven of your peace in this Bay State:
Neither my father nor his father. Beached
On these dry flats of fishy real estate,
O Mother, I implore
Your scorched, blue thunderbreasts of love to pour
Buckets of blessings on my burning head
Until I rise like Lazarus from the dead:
Lavabis nos et super nivem dealbabor.

"On Copley Square I saw you hold the door
To Trinity, Kingsolving's Church, and saw
The painted Paradise of harps and lutes
Sink like Atlantis in the Devil's jaw
And knock the Devil's teeth out by the roots;
But when I strike for shore
I find no painted idols to adore:
Hell is burned out, heaven's harp-strings are slack.
Mother, run to the chalice, and bring back
Blood on your finger-tips, for Lazarus who was poor."

In the disparate images of this section of the poem, theology, liturgy, mythology, history, and personal observation are fused. The "clippers" and "slavers" of the first stanza are meant to suggest the materialistic exploitation of one's fellowman which Lowell associates with the decay of Christianity and the evils of capitalism. This decay—"Kingsolving's Church," painted like the city of Babylon in Apocalypse 18:22—must sink like Atlantis, the materialistic paradise of yore, into the Devil's jaw, which has been the source of the material prosperity and religious decay of the world and, by sinking, knock the Devil's teeth out by the roots. The sinking is to be followed by a brief period of death, to approximate perhaps the four days of Lazarus' death or the three days of Christ's, in which the speaker "finds no painted idols to adore: / Hell is burned out, heaven's harp-strings are slack."

To anyone conversant with Apocalypse or classical mythol-

17

ogy this sinking will defeat the Devil, for teeth are regenerative organs. The incident in its idea of reaping salvation out of destruction seems culled in particular from the legend of the golden fleece, where Jason, in order to get the golden fleece, must first plant and then reap the harvest of his crop of dragon's teeth. The fleece by both its color and lamb-origin signifies Christ, and the comparison, a popular one in *Land of Unlikeness*, repeats itself elsewhere in the volume.

Opposed to these images of decay are the poem's images of salvation. The speaker will rise like Lazarus from the flood. This, as Lazarus' sister Martha explains, is to be on the last day: "I know that he will rise at the resurrection, on the last day" (John 11:24). When he does, he will sing the asperges hymn, reminding all Catholics of their baptismal vows. It is the same hymn which Dante's late repentants sing in *Purgatorio*. Being moreover a variation of the liturgical *lavabo* chant, recited previous to the consecration of the Holy Eucharist, the hymn prepares the reader for the Eucharistic symbolism of the second stanza when Lowell asks Mary to "run to the chalice, and bring back / Blood on your finger-tips, for Lazarus who was poor." Christ, having been reinstated in the poem as the Eucharist, is restored to Lazarus and the world, who were poor or poorer without Him. The image, a reversal of the fate assigned to Lazarus in Luke (16:24), puts the rich man in heaven. It may be intended to reflect again on the "black Swan" uniqueness of Winslow's fate.

One recognizes immediately the shift in this section from a concern with death and resurrection to an emphasis on the sacraments of life, baptism and Holy Eucharist. This shift exists without any significant structural changes from the previous parts of the cycle. The inverse baroque is there, and François Villon's "Ballade—Que Villon Feist à la Request de sa Mère, Pour Prier Nostre Dame" as well as Apocalypse 18:22 has added "The painted Paradise of harps and lutes." What thematic substance the poem contains lies, as usual, in the closing lines of each stanza, and what meaning there is is filtered through the cultural and religious backgrounds of the poet.

The only real confusion of the poem arises in its failure to construct the event concretely. This failure is most noticeable in the relationship of the poem's observations to the position of the speaker and may reflect on the contemplative direction of the poem. In the opening stanza the speaker is "beached," and in the second, he is "striking for shore." This confusion lessens if one realizes that what Lowell asks for in the poem is not an acceptance of an ordered world, but an abundance of blessing and an actual flood to come and destroy world chaos, first by washing away its sinners and then by rebaptizing it. For this reason Mary is said to have "thunderbreasts of love." "Thunderbreasts" suggest the Apocalyptic angel with the open scroll of God's promises and powers; and "breasts" convey the mystical Ideal against whose bosom the mystic submerges himself. In this manner, Mary is to signify both the destruction and salvation of the world.

Thus, what Tate meant in calling Lowell "consciously a Catholic poet" is that Lowell has consciously chosen a position of aesthetic involvement which can merge the techniques of religious vision with those of artistic vision. Behind this choice is the belief that God, not man, is the measure of ultimate reality and that what is important about man is not his achievements but his soul, his likeness to God. In such a relationship the function of the poet, like that of the prophet, is to reveal essential reality to the world which may have lost sight of it. He is no longer the imitator of life in the Aristotelian sense; he is the illuminator of Joyce's *Portrait* or Dante's *Divine Comedy*.

Nevertheless, in the cycle's tendency to combine pagan and Christian theology, one can understand the reservations any reader may have to Lowell's being a Catholic poet, for the tendency casts a foreboding shadow over the world Lowell is beginning to examine. Like Dante, he seems to take his heroes and epic events from Vergil, Lucan, and Ovid, and like Dante, he merges these heroes and events into a structure of Christian morality. The result is not always happy, for, as a poet, he can develop modern counterparts to Aeneas and still be forced to condemn them theologically. Ulysses, for instance, ends up in Dante's *Inferno* in the circle reserved for evil counselors. In addition, there is a whole realm of twentieth-century experience which Lowell seems not able to examine—or to examine only with distortion—because there are no exact classical parallels.

CHAPTER TWO

Land of Unlikeness

Land of Unlikeness (1944) presents Lowell's first panoramic look at a world where, as Allen Tate remarked, there is a "memory of the spiritual dignity of man now sacrificed to mere secularization and a craving for mechanical order." The title of the book, a translation of St. Bernard's *regio dissimilitudinis*, parallels the idea of its inscription, also from St. Bernard: *Inde anima dissimilis Deo / Inde dissimilis est et sibi* ("As the soul is unlike God, so too is it unlike itself"). The unlikeness, an unlikeness to God and to man's former self, is presented in both its religious and historical natures throughout the book. Its presentation, in addition, echoes the sentiments of Jean C. de Mènasce, whose articles were then appearing in *The Commonweal* (1940–44): "The church of the ill-willed, Hobbes's Leviathan, covers the whole earth." Its imagery also derives much from de Mènasce's work.

The purposes of the book are several: to explain the nature of the soul and to show both how it becomes unlike God and how it can regain His likeness. As a result, most of the poems, while remaining epical in structure, are expository, didactic, and critical. Modern man is seen repeatedly in comparison with Lowell's saved figure (St. Bernard) or Lowell's Christian figure (Christian Pilgrim); Lowell's lapsed Christian (Faust) or Lowell's damned figure (Cain); and the nature of his soul is repeatedly defined as love. Moreover, the reader discovers that the degree of the soul's likeness to God determines the degree of its free will, for in the tradition of many theologians, Lowell believes that free will is the power to choose right and that the grace one has aids in this selection. In the case of mortal sin, the ability to choose right is meaningless, for man's spiritual life is entirely conditioned. Thus by sinning, man loses not only his likeness to God, but also the spiritual benefits of right choice. Consequently, of the figures, St. Bernard represents the figure with most choice—the most truly free man—and Cain the most determined.

The means of regaining God's likeness are also made clear in the book. After the original gaining of likeness in baptism, a man may augment this likeness as St. Bernard did, through Christian love, mysticism, devotion to the Virgin Mary, and good works. Or, like Arthur Winslow, he may augment it through a complete faith in Christ, an avoidance of war, a belief in the power of prayer, and an ability to value worldly goods at no more than their price. Regardless of how the likeness is augmented, the remaining figures, with the exception of St. Bernard who functions on a completely contemplative level, exist on levels which are human, historical, and time-possessed, and which, as in sections of "In Memory of Arthur Winslow," can be approached through the devices of meditation already outlined.

Since the book's intention of making the soul aware of the forces of determinism is principally corrective in nature, Lowell is primarily concerned in it with the figures of Faust, Pilgrim, and Cain. Rather than classical, all three are basically Christian prototypes. The first of these, Faust, is especially important to "The Park Street Cemetery," which opens the volume, as well as to such poems as "On the Eve of the Feast of the Immaculate Conception, 1942," and "The Bomber." As the lapsed Christian, he is the one who sets the tone of the volume.

In "The Park Street Cemetery" Lowell establishes his character as he takes modern man on an epic descent into the underworld of the Boston graveyard, where he encounters memories of the "stern surnames" of the founding fathers: "Adams, / Otis, Hancock, Mather, Revere; / Franklin's mother." These memories which "fascinated," like that Walpurgis Nacht instrumental in Faust's own fall from grace, parallel Faust's Walpurgis Nacht visit to the Pharsalian Fields in Part II of Goethe's play, only here little is to be recovered from the descent. Man finds only the fickleness and transience of history. The world which has settled *in saecula saeculorum* has not only forgotten its dead, but it has forgotten as well what these dead fought to preserve—the new Canaan where man might again try to escape the corrupting influences of his surroundings.

Thus, this Faust in his thirst for power and deification has lost much more than his likeness to God; he has lost his spiritual imagination. In his hands, Adams, Mather, the material remains of the Puritan Dracos (harsh lawgivers as well as dragons), their stocks and Paradises become merely talismans for the resurrection of a destructive national pride. Through them, the speaker seeks only to revive the spiritual zeal which netted them their "filagreed swaths of forget-me-nots" and which might stimulate Americans into the war being fought, for all their names at one time or another were linked with war—Mather having worked to bring about King Philip's War, the others, the Revolutionary War.

Against these names and this descent, Lowell sets his image of likeness—"Easter crowds / On Boston Common." The meaning is clear: Those who live according to the flesh die. The Otises, Hancocks, Mathers, Reveres cannot see "the Irish hold the Golden Dome." Sacrificed to the sands of history, their hopes as well as their bones are represented by "frayed cables" and "the spreading obelisks." Catholicism holds the future of the world.

"On the Eve of the Feast of the Immaculate Conception, 1942" presents an alternative to this view of Faust and offers a second remedy to the situation posed in "The Park Street Cemetery." Condemning the then current evil of the world—world war—the poem entreats the "Mother of God, whose burly love / Turns swords to plowshares" to improve on "the big wars" by ending them and making her feast day a "holiday with Mars." By eliminating war, the poet hopes that the evil which prompts man's Faustian interests and powers over life and death will be removed. In addition, the temptation to fall farther away from God by becoming a Cain figure would be lessened.

The fear of destruction behind this hope, the fear of man's eventually turning through war into a Cain figure is Lowell's greatest fear, for it represents a betrayal of Christ, who died to establish a fellowship or brotherhood of man. It forces man from the principles of brotherhood into murder and thereby damns him. The fear of destruction prompts Lowell to call up the particular image in his address: "Six thousand years / Cain's blood has drummed into my ears." Aware, as well, of the effects of this lost Christian fellowship, an archetypal, determined pattern from

which man as Cain will not escape, Lowell entreats Mary again to
appeal to these soldiers to reconsider their position:

> *Oh, if soldiers mind you well*
> *They shall find you are their belle*
>   *And belly too;*
> *Christ's bread and beauty came by you.*

But all is not bleak. As "the Irish" closed the previous poem, this
poem, too, closes on an image of hope, for far away and across the
sea, the world of peace is revealed as another Israel, where the
Mother of God, like the Biblical hunter Nimrod, dances on Mars-
turned-Satan's head, and "Man eats the Dead / From pole to pole."

"The Bomber" outlines the ugliness of war, which abuses its
God-like methods of destruction; in this poem there are no images
of hope. Cain has arrived, and there can be no salvation for individuals who by their natures leave shattered bodies the souls of which,
because they lie in unconsecrated ground, cannot enter heaven.
These sentiments embody Lowell's violent opposition to "total
bombing," the 1942–45 all-out Allied offensive which made little
distinction in its targets between military and civilian objectives.
They form an indictment against the Faustian pilots of the planes
who have assumed a power they cannot control. In time, like the
sinners of Sodom and Gomorrah, they will have to account for
their moral failures.

In the poem these moral failures have, for the time being,
turned the "noonday night." The change reflects St. Bernard's *Sermons on "The Song of Songs,"* from which Lowell gets both the
title and inscription for *Land of Unlikeness*. There the "noonday"
is associated with Christ and "night" with Satan. Thus, the world
left to such bombings becomes diabolic rather than Christian, and
Faust, as he is at the end of most versions of the legend, is damned,
not saved.

Stylistically each of the three poems is stiff, didactic, and uncompromising. If, as inferred, the purpose of the meditational
structure is not to proselytize but to bring life to the surroundings,
it has failed here. All the same, the poems do form the core of one
major figure of *Land of Unlikeness*, the Faust-Cain prototype.
This prototype, using Faust's scientific means to achieve power,
achieves unlikeness to God and falls into Cain when this power is
employed to do physical violence. Science and war pose great
threats to man's salvation by tempting him most from his religious

imagination and his likeness to God. These threats become increasingly more significant and damaging as man falls farther from likeness.

A second recurrent figure in the book is Christian Pilgrim. This prototype, based on John Bunyan's *The Pilgrim's Progress*, images the modern hero in the miry Slough of Despond and pictures primarily his temptations and his occasional falls from grace. When he appears, he is easily identified by the "bog-slough" imagery of his surroundings. Like Christian and Christiana, he must conquer this Slough if he is to reach the Celestial City. But before he does, his realization of his lost condition and the scum and filth about him will produce many fears, doubts, and discouraging apprehensions. In *Land of Unlikeness*, this stage of his journey seems to interest Lowell most.

"A Suicidal Nightmare," the first of his appearances, is a dream dialogue which recalls the seventeenth-century dialogues of soul and body. Here the "soul" is the cowardly "tiger of the gutless heart," and its opponent is the speaker of the poem. Both reflect on a maimed man "stooping with his bag," while they are traveling in a borrowed car near a swamp. "Heart" prophesies that murder—"Cain's nine and outcast lives"—is the man's burden. This prophecy is believed by the speaker who, watching the man, goes off the road into the bog. The accident produces a new awareness which releases the fears of his heart to his consciousness. This release sends the speaker into the lower bog (the Slough of Despond), where he is helped out by the maimed man, who stops and slings him on his back. From this event, the speaker realizes that knowledge can conquer fear.

"Scenes from the Historic Comedy," the other of his appearances, demonstrates again by its title—as opposed to Dante's *Divine Comedy*—that most of the poems in the book concern themselves with the human, time-possessed, and definite. In Part One, entitled "Slough of Despond," the fears and doubts of Pilgrim predictably form the conditions of the section. "Pursey" suggests the sensual, materialistic nature of his sin.

The means, however, which the poet finds for the hero's crossing the swamp differ from the faith of Bunyan's heroes. The means here are a physical sign of religion, a religious article. Shouldering this religious article gives the hero the ability and strength to become temporarily like Alexander the Great, possessor of the East or anywhere he desires. Unfortunately, it cannot free him from his surroundings and his need for physical signs: "Lax / And limp, the creepers caught me by the foot, / And then I toed their line."

Pictured in the closing stanza is man's only way to regain his salvation, complete faith in Christ, which will permit him to walk like Winslow on the crest of the world-ending flood through the dunghills about him. The Dead Sea, traditionally placed at the center of the Last Judgment, is swelling. Christ is downed by the anti-Christ: "The bats of Babel"—modern civilization—flap about Japan, "the rising sun of Hell."

The picture of the end of modern civilization is enlarged in Parts Two and Three of the poem. Part Two, "The Fall of Babylon," based on Apocalypse 18–19, depicts the destruction of materialism, "the whore of Babylon." Part Three, "From Palestine's Inferno," shows an overview of Palestine, glimpsed as Dante's purgatorial view of the Inferno. It reveals the war in Africa, the charred planes blazing "manmarks" from the world man never created, the British hunting Field Marshal Erwin Rommel, "the desert fox." In contrast to these scenes, the poem offers mysticism as the final fire of love to withstand the returning barbarism of Mithra, Europa, and the setting sun.

For both Lowell's Faust and Pilgrim, the outward forces of history, particularly materialism, are important. Man's salvation can be aided by a Christian community, just as his damnation may be encouraged by an un-Christian environment. This second, Lowell feels, is the current situation. As de Mènasce expresses the idea: "We are suffering today because moral man . . . is held prisoner in the network of an immoral society. . . . We must have a society with a Catholic framework." Protestant liberty has handed man "over, bound hand and foot, to the tyranny of Great Men, to all the fancies and the systems of professors, experts and geniuses."

The nature of this network of immoral society is described in Lowell's two sonnets, "Salem" and "Concord," and in "Christmas Eve in the Time of War." It includes the loss of stature in man as well as creeping materialism. "Salem," as Lowell summarized for a *Life* magazine reporter, "is a lament for dead sailors and for the past greatness of the port of Salem." "Concord," on the other hand, is Lowell's attack on "Mammon's unbridled industry." "Christmas Eve in the Time of War" pictures again the destruction of materialism in the Apocalypse.

In "Salem," the opening lines present an image of a sailor, half-asleep and dreaming as he works with a knitting needle, reminded by spindrift of fleets of ships. The poem then pictures his dream, the slick of a sunken ship and the dead sailors floating on the oily water. These sailors, the "damned goods" of the poem, are left by Charon, who as one learned in "In Memory of Arthur Winslow" is to load the souls of the faithful in port and send them out to meet their Savior, the "fisherman" Christ. As a consequence, the souls of these sailors sicken in the seas and the sailor is reminded of the more heroic fleets that once sailed the Great Banks. In the last line the dreamer mourns the passing of Salem's famous whalers and the privateers who fought the British to their knees.

Taken at its literal level, the action of the poem becomes mere jingoism; closely read, the poem gains in significance. The eighteenth-century British lion embodies the principles of colonialism, mercantilism, and the exploitation of one's fellowman. By opposing the British, the Salem forebears strike an important blow against these practices and thereby bring the lion to his knees. This significance—more often than patriotism—is intended in the recurrent Puritan images.

"Concord," named for the town which marked the beginning of the Revolutionary War, extends the theme of mercantilism and exploitation to our own time and attacks the generally unchristian attitude in American industry. In light of a later change to "Ford," "gold" in its opening line typifies the unchristian attitude poised, as the poem suggests, and searching time for its continuity.

In the poem the continuity is one of opposites, of Minute Men, Irish Catholics, Concord Bridge, Walden Pond, Unitarianism, and Catholicism. Finally, in this generally Heraclitean flux, it becomes the conflict of crucifix and Mammon, the crucifix which has tried to join men in peace and Mammon which separates them by war. This final opposition situated at Concord, one of the centers of Unitarianism, returns the opposition to its beginnings. Thus, in a series of post hoc associations, Lowell sums up his ideas. Unitarianism has destroyed the achievements of that war by "washing out" the significance of Christ's death. It provided the philosophy which industrialists used to exploit their fellowman. Modern man, by his greed for gold and his deeds of exploitation, stands opposed to his former state, when he had fought a wilderness and a war to abolish others' exploitation of himself.

"Christmas Eve in the Time of War" brings the reader back to war as a source of man's unlikeness to God and his former self and to money again as the source of the war. In the poem, a laissez-faire capitalist stands by a Civil War monument and meditates on the state of the world during a Christmas eve blackout. The past which had managed to solve everything with money, even the fear of Hell, is now faced with an uncompromising present:

> *Tonight the venery of capital*
> *Hangs the bare Christ-child on a tree of gold,*
> *Tomorrow Mars will break his bones.*

In the industrialist's thought, the line of statues erected to war heroes becomes a colonnade to world destruction. These statues have "ridden the whirlwinds" of God's wrath and "directed the drums"—actions which in Apocalypse, St. John associates with the end of man. Thinking that he might be able to buy off this destruction, the capitalist appeals to the materialistic gods of Santa Claus and Hamilton "to break the price-controller's strangle-hold."

The Christ-child, however, comes with water and fire, the elements of mankind's total ruin. The capitalist knows it is "no use" and asks the statued generals if they tremble, for the "ruler knows his own Star," and disavows the pretorians. Again the avenging Savior of Armageddon, Christ announces, " 'I bring no peace, I bring the sword, . . . / My nakedness was fingered and defiled.' " The capitalist, who has been one of this doubting group of moderns, warns in his last line: "Woe unto the rich that are with child."

All three poems stress man's unlikeness with his former self and represent what would be the "Babylon" of the unchristian network of society rather than the Catholic in Lowell. Together they form Lowell's entirely social "economic view" of America. With Pound, for whom he had great admiration, Lowell feels the failure of America is basically tied to her economic structure. This failure, both poets root in the government's continual protection of the manufacturer and financier at the cost of the public. They trace support for their ideas to President Martin Van Buren. Feeling that the "money interest had compelled the Government to be its [sic] servant, to loan to them its revenue, to connect itself with commercial exchanges," Van Buren fought to get the government out of banking and independent of banks and bankers. He paid for his fight in 1840 when the "money interest" succeeded in electing

William Henry Harrison President. The government remained in banking, trusting for its stability to the wisdom of these bankers, enacting legislation for their benefit.

Henry Adams, in his *Education,* describes the culmination of this move with the acceptance of the single gold standard: "For a hundred years, between 1793 and 1893, the American people had hesitated, vacillated, swayed forward and back, between two forces, one simply industrial, the other capitalistic, centralizing and mechanical. In 1893, the issue came on the single gold standard, and the majority at last declared itself, once and for all, in favor of the capitalistic system with all its necessary machinery." Trusting to the wisdom of bankers had, in some minds, led first to the depression of the 1930's and finally to World War II. This principle of American economics had to be revoked:

> *Here Yankee laissez-faire and enterprise*
> *Build pyres on expiation to the night*
> *The rising sun of aping Japanese*
> *Blazes upon the Democratic twilight,*
> *Old ironsides shatter the Pacific Seas.*

Its revocation might lead to some other economic system, perhaps to the Christian anarchy advocated by Lowell's friends on *The Catholic Worker.* In such a system, laissez-faire capitalism would give way to considerations of more permanent value than gold and war.

"Napoleon Crosses the Beresina," which follows the sonnets, is Lowell's moral on what happens when, as a consequence of such an economic theory, nations put too much emphasis on war. Napoleon's disastrous retreat across the steppes is turned into a sermon in which Christ's words form the inscription, "And wheresoever you see Eagles, look for the bodies" (Matthew 24:28). Christ, who is speaking of the Last Day, describes this end of the world as if it were a war. The image of the eagle fits nicely into the Napoleonic scene and suggests that this retreat stands in a Judgment Day relationship to Napoleon and his dying men.

What Lowell seems to indicate is that all wars are alike. Napoleon is "Charlemagne's stunted shadow." Hitler, in turn, is another Napoleon. This statement, along with Lowell's other views, suggests a recurrent historical pattern which is quite important in more than its archetypal basis. It implies a cyclical view of history which is more Greek than Catholic. In principle, it implies that certain historical situations recur of necessity and pattern. Although such a theory is good for his epical view of poetry, it would confer, if realized, a degree of determinism and lack of free will on the mechanics of history. This determinism would be most disastrous to those whose likeness to God has already been diminished.

Thus the subject matter of the poem again demands that the poet be harshly critical of his principals. The indictments are the same as Ezekiel and Joel pronounce upon their cultures, toward a similar end—shaming and frightening their audiences back to God's likeness. They have the same unrelenting firmness that Christ had toward the money changers. Religion is not to be desecrated or saved by namby-pamby methods. It is conceived in militancy and requires continual militancy to keep it going. As St. Matthew expresses it, "The kingdom of heaven suffereth violence, and the violent bear it away" (Matthew 11:12).

The presence of this view of history is made even clearer in the murderer images in the volume's closing pages. These images emphasize Cain as the major figure of man's unlikeness to God and prompted Lloyd Frankenberg to suggest in *Pleasure Dome* (Boston, 1949) that Lowell is another of the New England writers haunted by the spirits of America's murdered Indians. "The Crucifix," "Children of Light," and "Leviathan" hark back to earlier poems, except that what were poetic patterns of free will have now become compulsive, determined, ritualistic actions. As such, the lessening free will of the poems suggests a dangerous extension of the cyclical idea of history from "Napoleon Crosses the Beresina," and although they do not embrace this view fully enough to become nearly blasphemous, they offer the bleakest view of man in the volume.

The first of these poems, "The Crucifix," has the poet ask how he is to escape the Cain role which man continually acts, for he recognizes that blood leads only to more blood.

> *Adam, if our land*
> *Become the incarnation of a hand*
> *That shakes the Temple back to clay, how can*
> *War ever change my old into new man?*

Everyone, including Adam, is too intent upon saving his own life from impending doom to answer the question. The poet, the poem's "stray dog," finds his answer and direction in the image of the Crucifix.

"Children of Light" is bleaker in outlook. It harks back to Cotton Mather and King Philip's War (1675–77). Prompted by Lowell's forebear, Josiah Winslow, then governor of Plymouth, the Pilgrims waged war successfully and unjustifiably against the Indian King Philip. As presented to the people of New England by their clergy, the war was a religious war: God called on His Elect to defeat the forces of evil. Seemingly Lowell takes up the cry of the oppressed Indians from sentiments like those of Quaker John Easton's conclusion to *A Relacion of the Indyan Warre:* "I am so perswaided of new England prists thay ar so blinded by the spiret of persecution and to maintaine to have hyer, and to have rume to be mere hyerlings that they have bine the Case that the law of nations and the law of arems have been voiolated in this war." Lowell turns this cry into a satirical and pregnant poem the opening of which echoes lines from Milton's "On the Late Massacre in Piedmont." Massacres as well as wars repeat themselves, and both the Pilgrims and their descendants are Cain figures who formed the boundaries of their properties with murdered Redmen's bones.

The only "light" in the poem comes from the "Serpent's seeds of light," which the Pilgrims planted. These are the seeds in Matthew (13:5–6) which fell upon rocky ground. They are now being burned by the blood of Cain. As in the parable, they signify those who have heard and accepted God's Word, yet who could not withstand tribulations and persecutions. These tribulations and persecutions create a "hall of mirrors," perhaps Versailles, whose treaties of peace have not worn well.

"Leviathan," which concludes the volume, carries the Cain-Abel analogy to the present. Both its title and basic imagery derive from the opening sentence of Hobbes's famous treatise on materialism and government: "By art is created that great Leviathan, called a Commonwealth or State—(in Latin, *civitas*) which is but an artificial man." Concerned with the political and moral obligations of that state in war, the poem describes the commonwealth as man's way of atoning for Abel by learning to live peacefully with his fellowman. In war, it forfeits this function: "The Ship / Of State is asking Christ to walk on blood." Nevertheless, God's perpetual beneficence will, as in the past, provide a means of man's escape:

> *When Israel turned from God's wise fellowship,*
> *He sent us Canaan or Exile, Ark or Flood,*

At last, for brotherhood,
Our Savior and His saving Heart.

The definition of this means of escape forms a large part of the
remaining poems of the volume, for Lowell's vision includes not
only a view of corruption but also a pattern of salvation. He feels
inwardly that his chances of being saved will be increased if he can
destroy the conditions in "Napoleon Crosses the Beresina" and
"The Bomber" which exist about man, tempting him into unlikeness. These conditions are much like the "Jerusalem" of the Old
Testament prophets, not really places, but aspects of American
morality. They never signal the complete destruction of mankind,
for Babylon-Boston produces as well the conditions for likeness.
"In Memory of Arthur Winslow" presents some of these conditions with its "black swan" image. "A Suicidal Nightmare" presents another of them with "knowledge."

"The Drunken Fisherman" presents more conditions of likeness. Half-reprobate, half-philosopher, the fisherman of the poem
is pictured as potentially a microcosmic replica of Christ, the
Man-fisher. The underlying metaphor suggests "imitation of
Christ" as a way of augmenting likeness. Thus, all the images and
actions of the poem take on symbolic importance. The river, a
"bloody sty," is the world at war. "Jehovah's bow," representing
God's hopeful covenant with man, "suspends no pots of gold," the
materialism of man. The "blood-mouthed trout"—those willing to
make sacrifices—rise to the fisherman and so to God, except that
this microcosmic fisherman, unlike the theological Man-fisher, has
only a temporary catch: "They flopped about / My canvas creel
until the moth / Corrupted its unstable cloth." Finally, the fisherman asks, "Is there no way to cast my hook / Out of this dyna-
mited brook?" and is told: "The Fisher's sons must cast about /
When shallow waters peter out." He is determined to cast about
for Christ and catch Him before his death, knowing that somehow
Christ is connected with this stream. Thus, as did Henry David
Thoreau in "The Ponds" section of *Walden*, the fisherman of
Lowell's poem attempts his likeness to God by disregarding the
war being fought about him and by coming to terms with nature
and himself. This inner peace Lowell seems to feel is most important to salvation, for as Thoreau remarked, man must start his
reformation with himself. If he waits for his fellowman, he may
never begin.

"Dea Roma," a history of Rome from Augustus to the present, reenforces Catholicism as a condition for salvation. In the world of fading Christianity, Rome is still the Eternal City, and Christ still walks the waters of her rivers to the Celestial City of Heaven. In fact, like Dante, only from the "dry Dome" of St. Peter's can the souls of the faithful leave to meet Christ. This dry dome, Michelangelo's sublime masterpiece, which time has colored gold, complements the "golden" Statehouse dome of "The Park Street Cemetery."

These poems suggest that modern man should pay careful attention to the qualities which helped to save Arthur Winslow's soul. To them Lowell has added Catholicism, knowledge, imitation of Christ, and mysticism. Nevertheless, for anyone emotionally engaged in fighting a war and to whom Hitler is pictured as the Devil incarnate, the sentiments of this first volume seem vindictive and nearly traitorous. To ask for fellowship and peace and to attack war and capitalism in the midst of such a struggle for existence seem to place superhuman demands upon one's fellowman. In addition, there are important shortcomings in the volume's technique. Conrad Aiken in *The New Republic* (1944) lists some of them: "Here and elsewhere in his book, Mr. Lowell's undercurrent of fierce satire contributes an immense vigor and gusto. . . . When this slackens, however, the verse tends to become either turgid and strained or merely heraldic, and the thematic limitations more manifest." Other shortcomings are rooted in the meditational structure which Lowell has attempted to use. If he has real vision of "the disappearance of the Christian experience from the modern world," he is not able to convey this as such. He seems to have merely a notional assent to it. He dogmatically believes in Apocalypse, but he cannot yet imagine the events in terms which are vivid enough for good epical poetry. He seems merely a young man in a library using the Bible as a source book for poetry. As R. P. Blackmur remarks of this failure in *The Kenyon Review* (1945): "It is as if he demanded *to know* (to judge, to master) both the substance apart from the form with which he handles it and the form apart from the substance handled in order to set them fighting. . . . and the fight produces not a tension but a gritting. It is not the violence, the rage, the denial of this world that grits, but the failure of these to find *in verse* a tension of necessity."

CHAPTER THREE

The Contemplative Voice

The panoramic view of *Land of Unlikeness* also provides in its figure of St. Bernard more overt indications of the contemplative directions of Lowell's verse. These indications, already mentioned in the discussion of "In Memory of Arthur Winslow," extend to such poems as "Cistercians in Germany" as well as the later "The Quaker Graveyard in Nantucket," "The North Sea Undertaker's Complaint," "Colloquy in Black Rock," and "Mary Winslow." Like the title and inscription for *Land of Unlikeness*, the direction derives from St. Bernard and his principal commentator, St. Bonaventure: "We have among us Martha . . . in those who faithfully discharge our temporal affairs; we have Lazarus . . . in our novices who . . . still go in fear of judgement till the assurance of Christ's pardon rolls away the stone. . . . And we have also contemplative Mary."

As previously explained, the direction differs from the meditational exercises of St. Ignatius in two respects: first, in that it seeks anagogic truth (God) as its ends; and second, in that its ecstasy, unlike that of the meditational exercise, withdraws from sensuous images. The meditational exercise, which sought at best to make its practitioners an experiential part of the life of Christ and the joys of Heaven, had been "human, time-possessed, and definite." Contemplation extends into what Father Lynch calls "escape-theology"; its whole direction is toward a mystical union with God and a subsequent burning out of all experience.

In 1943, the year before *Land of Unlikeness*, Lowell expressed an interest in this particular direction in a review of T. S. Eliot's *Four Quartets:* "My own feeling is that union with God is somewhere in sight in all poetry, though it is usually rudimentary and misunderstood." He views the Eliot poems as "the most remarkable and ambitious expression of Catholic mysticism in English" as well as "something of a community product." The term "Catholic mysticism" reveals part of what Lowell means by "union with God," but his note on Gerard Manley Hopkins, a year later, adds substantially to an understanding of what this "mysticism" is:

> Like other practiced writers, Hopkins was able to use most of his interests and experiences in his poetry. However, if we compare him with his peers . . . , we see that he was able to do this rather more than others. Why? . . . they mused, they fabled, they preached, they schemed and they damned. Hopkins is substantially dramatic (*in act* according to the language of scholastic philosophy).

> . . . What I want to emphasize is that for Hopkins, life was a continuous substantial progress toward perfection. He believed this, he lived this, this is what he wrote.

This "mysticism" is what Bonaventure describes in his *Meditations on the Life of Christ* (St. Louis, 1934) as the second part of the active life: "By these two sisters the Saints understood the two modes of life, active and contemplative. . . . There is the first life represented by Martha. As I gather from Blessed Bernard's teaching, there are in the active life two parts. The first part is that in which a soul exercises herself chiefly in correcting herself. . . . The second part of the active life is spent in doing good actively to the neighbour. . . . Between these two parts of the active life there is the contemplative life." The active life is possible, then, only after the "union with God" of the contemplative life. To achieve it, Lowell must first seek an escape theology.

Here certain steps must be observed. George Bosworth Burch sums them up in his Introduction to Saint Bernard's *The Steps of Humility* (Cambridge, Mass., 1942): "These, then, are the three steps of the anagogic path: humility, love, and contemplation. They lead respectively to knowledge of truth in yourself, knowl-

edge of truth in your neighbor, and knowledge of Truth itself."
More important for a reader of Lowell's poetry is how these steps
once achieved are manifested in a work of art. St. Bernard provides
the clue to this: "And let us seek, if you will, those three things in
Holy Scripture—a garden, a storeroom and a bedchamber. . . .
And so let the *garden* be the simple and plain historic sense. Let the
storeroom be the moral sense. Let the *bedchamber* be the secret of
interior contemplation." Thus, the contemplative poem, of its own
nature seeks a multilevel interpretation, and this is suggested in
Tate's Introduction to *Land of Unlikeness* by the references to religious, personal, and historical poems.

"Cistercians in Germany," the only poem besides "Death from
Cancer" in *Land of Unlikeness* to strive consciously toward the
multilevel view, describes the spiritual descendants of St. Bernard
as they are persecuted by the Nazis:

> *Here corpse and soul go bare. The Leader's headpiece*
> *Capers to his imagination's tumblings;*
> *The Party barks at its unsteady fledglings*
> *To goose-step in red-tape, and microphones*
> *Sow the four winds with babble.*

The Nazis, whose microphones sow "the four winds with babble,"
sow the destruction of mankind and the end of the world. The
"red dragon" of Apocalypse appears to "lick up Jesus' blood."
"Valhalla," the pagan heaven of Germany's warriors and of Nazi
patriotism, "vapors from the punctured tank."

> *Rank upon rank the cast-out Cistercians file*
> *Unter den Linden to the Wilhelmsplatz,*
> *Where Caesar paws the gladiator's breast;*
> *His martial bumblings and hypnotic yawp*
> *Drum out the pastors of these aimless pastures. . . .*

The plight of these drummed-out "pastors" is pictured as it
affects uncomprehending, "moral" America. Its terms are reminiscent of the pastoral elegies of John Milton and Matthew Arnold
when both poets asked: Who is to pipe the shepherd's death?

> *But who will pipe of pastors, herds and hirelings*
> *Where a strait-laced mechanic calls the tune?*

Here the stamped tabloid, ballot, draft or actress
Consumes all access and all faculties
For spreading blandishments or terror.

If, as Lowell concludes, no one will pipe the story, the United States is unconcerned; God is not: "The Shepherd knows his sheep have gone to market; / Sheep need no pastoral piping for the kill, / Only cold mutton and a fleecing." What war and the United States will achieve is a retribution (repayment), not a remission (cancellation), and Lowell points out that a material retribution does not always lead to an end to Cain.

The last stanza indicts the Germans, "who have forgotten Adam's fault," the Original Sin which first established man's unlikeness to God, and suggests Lowell's plan for spiritual remission. Adam, having "sowed the dragon's teeth" of the German race, has sowed "ill for his descent." The pagan Junkers have destroyed the Christian cells, their means of salvation. The monks who must be saved lift their hands to "wizened Bernard," their founder and Dante's final guide in *Paradiso,* asking him to show them the way to achieve remission of sin and God's likeness. Bernard, who at once is both the mystical bridal chamber fresh with flowers and the ecstatic womb through which the sudden Bridegroom will appear, furnishes them with their answer. Through the contemplative "return to the womb" which he represents, the monks can prepare for both their salvation and their immortality.

Implicit in this standard contemplative image is a fuller picture of the true nature of Lowell's cyclical view of history. This view of history incorporates a Jungian archetypal patterning, basic to Lowell's choice of "epical form" as the form of his poetry. According to the Jungian view there are recurrent psychic types in history, and man's unconscious nature, caught up in a moment of time, adheres to these typal patterns. However, man need not be completely caught up in time. He may escape into psychical immortality and salvation. The Cistercians of the poem accomplish this by their archetypal "return to the womb"—"And all his body one extatic womb"—through mysticism and by being reborn. Baptism, in effect, serves this purpose in the structure of Christian sacraments: "Unless a man be born again, he cannot see the kingdom of God" (John 3:3). More primitive pagan means to this end, psychologists infer, are insanity and incest.

This psychical "means of escape from time" is in essence different from what Lowell implied when he wrote in "Leviathan" that God continually furnishes man with a method of achieving His likeness and salvation and that man need only to accept it. The psychical means is ultimately independent of salvation which with God's grace may be achieved "in time," for included in the means are escapes from time such as incest and insanity which have no relationship with God's likeness. Lowell, however, is not always careful to preserve these distinctions. He seems to make "escape from time," regardless of its purpose, the aim of many of his heroes.

Nevertheless, unlike "In Memory of Arthur Winslow," "Cistercians in Germany" fails to progress beyond the second, or moral level of meaning into anagogic Truth. Nowhere is there conveyed the presence of the union of man and God which occurs in the "Death from Cancer" and "A Prayer for My Grandfather to Our Lady" sections of the earlier poem. This poem stops precisely as the union is about to occur: "And through the trellis peers the sudden Bridegroom." Yet, because it gets this far, it must be separated from the overtly social and moral poems of the volume and considered as a not very successfully accomplished contemplative poem.

"The Quaker Graveyard in Nantucket," which appeared first in *Lord Weary's Castle* and which many critics cite as Lowell's best war poem, also partakes of the contemplative rather than the social and moral view. Written in memory of his cousin, Warren Winslow, whose ship had been torpedoed at sea, the poem outlines man's dominion on earth as assigned by God in Genesis (1:26): "Let man have dominion over the fishes of the sea and the fowls of the air and the beasts and the whole earth, and every creeping creature that moveth upon the earth." Its tension arises from that feeling of loss expressed by Herman Melville in *Moby Dick:* "What bitter blanks in those black-bordered marbles which cover no ashes! What despair in those immovable inscriptions! What deadly voids and unbidden infidelities in the lines that seem to gnaw upon all Faith, and refuse resurrections to the beings who have placelessly perished without a grave." Like the sailors of the "Pequod" in the epic quest for Moby Dick, the sea dead of the war, who quested for the Leviathan of State, will not return to port.

The poem begins after the torpedoing with a description of the finding of Winslow's remains in the North Atlantic. These remains, which are all that is left of Winslow's ship, symbolically take on the bloodless qualities of that vessel: "Its open, staring eyes / Were lustreless dead-lights / Or cabin-windows on a stranded hulk / Heavy with sand." As any remains turned up from the sea, they must be weighted down and sent back.

There Lowell pictures the body as being feasted upon by the "heel-headed" sharks whose progenitors once reduced Captain Ahab to a void. As befitting the dead, his name is "blocked in yellow chalk" before the body is released, taking Winslow's hopes and future with it. Its release "confesses / Its hell-bent deity," as Melville's "Pequod," "like Satan, would not sink to hell till she had dragged a living part of heaven along with her." Poseidon, "earth-shaker" and sea-god, needs to be faced by the sailors of the ship which found Winslow. Lowell warns them that when they are dead they will have "no Orphean lute / To pluck life back," merely the deadening "guns of the steeled fleet" recoiling and repeating "the hoarse salute."

As Hugh B. Staples has pointed out in *Robert Lowell: The First Twenty Years* (New York, 1962), the imagery of the first dozen lines is taken from the description of a shipwreck in the opening chapter of Henry David Thoreau's *Cape Cod:* "... the sea was still breaking violently on the rocks.... I saw many marble feet and matted heads as the clothes were raised, and one livid, swollen, and mangled body of a drowned girl...; the coiled-up wreck of a human hulk, gashed by the rocks or fishes, so that the bone and muscle were exposed, but quite bloodless,—merely red and white,—with wide-open and staring eyes, yet lustreless, dead-lights; or like the cabin windows of a stranded vessel, filled with sand."

Part II shifts to home port as the poem portrays the tensions of those left at home to await the return of loved ones from the sea. The sea which caused Winslow's death is frightening "to the fowls of the air." "The terns and sea-gulls tremble at your death." Their trembling conveys an indication of the disruption of the dominion given to man in Genesis. Lowell asks dead Winslow if he can hear "The Pequod's sea wings, beating landward, fall / Headlong and break ... / Off 'Sconset," where the American fleet is stationed for another "hell-bent" mission. The bones of the Quaker Graveyard in Nantucket are crying out for the hurt beast, Moby Dick, who, to Lowell, represents Christianity, "Bobbing by Ahab's whaleboats in the East." The use of the Quaker graveyard in preference to the New Bedford graveyard of Melville's *Moby Dick* is significant in that it emphasizes the essential Christian pacificism of the Quakers in light of the unchristian war.

Part III yields the significance of what has occurred in the previous parts. The warships are pictured as the sinners of Jonathan Edwards' famous sermon, "Sinners in the Hands of an Angry God." "Guns . . . rock / Our warships in the hand / Of the great God, where time's contrition blues / Whatever it was these Quaker sailors lost / In the mad scramble of their lives."

What these sailors lost is their secret. It is measured in their bones, not their souls, for only their bones inhabit the seas. Nevertheless, as "bluing" tends to make things whiter, the image echoes the asperges hymn of "In Memory of Arthur Winslow" and suggests they may be saved. This suggestion is reenforced when the relationship of Moby Dick and Christ is made more explicit. "IS" is called "the whited monster," and being thus capitalized is indicative of God. Moreover, the quick deaths of these Quaker sailors contrast with that slow acceptance of Winslow. In the sperm-whale's slick, the Atlantic rises quickly to swallow them up so that unlike the corpse of Part I they do not float about to be picked up by other ships nor need to be weighted in order to be swallowed by the sea. "If God himself had not been on our side, / If God himself had not been on our side, / When the Atlantic rose against us, why, / Then it had swallowed us up quick."

Part IV is a dirge for the death of Christianity. Christ, "the whale / Who spewed Nantucket bones on the thrashed swell / And stirred the troubled waters to whirlpools / To send the Pequod packing off to hell," is at His end as is the ocean, portrayed in her Old English kenning of "whaleroad" to suggest the time span of her supremacy. It is also the end of those sailors of modern war who "sail / Seaward and seaward on the turntail whale." The world is about to be destroyed. "This is the end of running on the waves," which in *Land of Unlikeness* is Lowell's means of going to heaven. Man is "poured out like water," again a soul symbol. The section ends with Lowell asking: "Who will dance / The mast-lashed master of Leviathans / Up from this field of Quakers in their unstoned graves?" Tashtego, "the mast-lashed master of Leviathans" and anti-Christ of Apocalypse must be removed from this world if it is to be saved.

As in the cetological digressions of *Moby Dick*, Part V deals with the disposal of the whale's rotting viscera. From what has come before, the reader recognizes that the description also applies to Christianity, the white whale having been identified with Christ. Lowell asks: When the whale's viscera go, will the sailor's sword whistle and fall and sink into the fat? When Christianity fails, will man be entirely reduced to a state of war? The poem then moves to "the great ash-pit of Jehoshaphat," cited by the prophet Joel as the place of the Last Judgment: "Let them arise, and let the nations come up into the valley of Jehoshaphat: for there I will sit to judge all nations round about" (Joel 3:12). There the "bones cry for the blood of the white whale," the blood of Christ's Crucifixion.

This "crucifixion" is seen as an echo of Stubb's killing of the whale in Chapter LXI of *Moby Dick*. The death lance of the whaler's harpoon "churns into the sanctuary," opening the sperm-whale's midriff. The churning produces the sperm-whale slick in which, in Part III, the Quakers drowned. Later, the image of the lance is repeated with the sinking figure of Ahab, this time as a variation of the famous "nail-key" pun of St. Bernard's portrayal of the Crucifixion: "But the piercing nail (*clavus*) has been turned for me into the master key (*clavis*), to show me the Will of the Lord." The repetition of the image at this new level indicates the shift Lowell is preparing between the moral and mystical levels of the poem.

The five parts also recall the pursuit of the Great Leviathan described by anthropologist Jessie L. Weston in *From Ritual to Romance* (Garden City, 1957): "What may be regarded as the central point of Jewish Fish symbolism is the tradition that, at the end of the world, Messias will catch the great Fish Leviathan, and divide its flesh as food among the faithful." In this case, the whale is not Christ, but "Jonas Messias," the container of Christ. It is death as described by Christ in Matthew (12:40): "For even as Jonas was in the belly of the fish three days and three nights, so will the Son of Man be three days and three nights in the heart of the earth." The proper piercing of the fish, consequently, would release Christ from his confinement, and the improper pursuit echo the sermon by Father Mapple in *Moby Dick*, describing the woe "of him whom this world charms from Gospel duty."

Part VI of "The Quaker Graveyard in Nantucket," "Our Lady of Walsingham," continues this shift from the moral to the mystical level. Based on Edward I. Watkin's description of the statue in *Catholic Art and Culture* (New York, 1944), the poem outlines almost word-for-word his account of this statue of "the Queen of Contemplatives." Its setting—

> ...where...pilgrims once took off their shoes to walk barefoot the remaining mile.... The road...a quiet country lane, shaded with trees and lined on one side by a hedgerow. On the other a stream flows...

—is transposed into the opening four lines of the section:

> *There once the penitents took off their shoes*
> *And then walked barefoot the remaining mile;*
> *And the small trees, a stream and hedgerows file*
> *Slowly along the munching English lane.*

Likewise, the symbolism of the stanza derives from Watkin. The stream in lines 7–9, flowing under the tree in Shiloah's whirlpools and making glad the castle of God, winds from this source: "On the other a stream flows down beneath the trees, the water symbol of the Holy Spirit, 'the waters of Shiloah that go softly,' the 'flow of the river making glad the city of God.' "

In stanza two, Lowell's description of Our Lady is a rearrangement of these quotations from Watkin:

> ...near an altar of medieval fashion, is seated Our Lady's image. It is too small for its canopy and is not superficially beautiful. *"Non est species neque decor"*; there is no comeliness or charm in that expressionless face with heavy eyelids.

> For centuries the shrine...has been an historical memory.

> That expressionless countenance expresses what is beyond expression.... For her spirit is in God, and she knows as He knows, receiving His knowledge. No longer the Mother of Sorrows nor yet of the human joy of the Crib....

Combined, they form the end of the section:

> *Our Lady, too small for her canopy,*
> *Sits near the altar. There's no comeliness*

At all or charm in that expressionless
Face with its heavy eyelids. As before,
This face, for centuries a memory,
Non est species, neque decor,
Expressionless, expresses God: it goes
Past castled Sion. She knows what God knows,
Nor Calvary's Cross nor crib at Bethlehem
Now, and the world shall come to Walsingham.

It is the last line which conveys the section's real significance. Taken from the following prediction in Watkin, the line parallels the view of man Lowell expressed in *Land of Unlikeness:*

> Our contemporaries worship power, the natural energy that drives machines and, on a higher level, is the life-force of animate things. Before the new world they desire can be born, they must learn the lesson Our Lady of Contemplation would teach us, that the power which alone can bring that new world to birth is supernatural, the power of God, the power that is also rest and silence, the power of contemplative prayer. In that sense, rather than in impressive statistics of conversions, will the saying prove true that when England goes to Walsingham, England will return to the Church. When the world goes thus to Walsingham, it will return to the Church. Nay, it will become the Church.

This is what the sailor of the opening stanza is doing, returning to Walsingham. Hence, the statue functions as Canaan, Exile, Ark, Flood, and Crucifix did in "Leviathan," as a means of escape from time into salvation and immortality.

The poet having achieved the harmony of mystical union and its vision, Part VII reexamines the world without the sinister effects of the earlier sections. "It's well," the poet says that the Atlantic is "fouled with the blue sailors, / Sea monsters, upward angel, downward fish." It is as the Lord wills. The Atlantic, which represents in her water not only the Holy Spirit but the history of man, has cast up Winslow as a lesson, as an example of sea-slime before God breathed life into it. The poem ends on a note of triumph: "The

Lord survives the rainbow of His will." God is still the awful and all powerful Lord of the Old Testament, existing as such despite any promise one thinks He has made not to use that power.

The rainbow, harking back to Genesis, suggests God's covenant with Noah after the Flood destroyed the corruption of the world: "I will set my bow in the clouds, and it shall be the sign of a covenant between me, and between the earth ... and there shall no more be waters of a flood to destroy all flesh" (Genesis 9:13-15). This covenant which restores the dominion of man set forth in the inscription also echoes the "new world" of Watkin in "Our Lady of Walsingham." It is the flooding baptism of the already discussed "A Prayer for My Grandfather to Our Lady" section of "In Memory of Arthur Winslow." It is God's covenant with Lowell's view of things.

The poem successfully demonstrates the contemplative direction. Written on three levels, it achieves in its closing sections the anagogic Truth which the contemplative exercise seeks. Its structure follows generally the steps of humility outlined by St. Bernard, beginning in the early sections with "knowledge of truth in himself" and ending with his idea of Truth itself. The poem manages, too, to express before its completion almost every theme and position in *Land of Unlikeness*, as well as the new covenant with God. Its only ideological disadvantage is its and Watkin's insistence that contemplation is the only method of achieving this new world. For any theologian this seems far too narrow a means of salvation. Even St. Bernard in his discussion of the need for contemplation could not go that far. He continually recognized the aid and necessity of Lazarus and Martha in the religious structure of things: The monk "should like Lazarus, be devoted to humble self-examination; although the more proficient monk may, like Mary, be devoted to contemplation, and the abbot must, like Martha, be devoted to the dispensative consideration."

Like "Cistercians in Germany," "The North Sea Undertaker's Complaint" deals with the death of religious persons during war. These religious persons are not being killed by the Nazis, in this instance, but by the phosphorus bombs dropped by the Allies in their "total bombings" of German-held territories. Relying heavily upon the reader's knowledge of Christian liturgy and mysticism to supply the shift from moral to mystical levels, the poem reads:

THE POETIC THEMES OF ROBERT LOWELL

> *Now south and south and south the mallard heads,*
> *His green-blue bony hood echoes the green*
> *Flats of the Weser, and the mussel beds*
> *Are sluggish where the webbed feet spanked the lean*
> *Eel grass to tinder in the take-off. South*
> *Is what I think of. It seems yesterday*
> *I slid my hearse across the river mouth*
> *And pitched the first iced mouse into the hay.*
> *Thirty below it is. I hear our dumb*
> *Club-footed orphan ring the Angelus*
> *And clank the bell-chain for St. Gertrude's choir*
> *To wail with the dead bell the martyrdom*
> *Of one more blue-lipped priest; the phosphorus*
> *Melted the hammer of his heart to fire.*

The shift in levels is centered in the meanings of "Angelus." The Angelus is both bell and the prayer which celebrates the Annunciation and the coming of Christ. Its mention prepares the reader for the mystical union contained in the final image of the poem, the phosphorus melting the heart. Coming after the mention of St. Gertrude, "Prophetess of the Sacred Heart" and thirteenth-century mystic, the image is reminiscent of St. Bernard's description of the true contemplative experience: "In truth, the fire which is God consumes, ... but it does not destroy. It burns sweetly. It leaves one desolate unto bliss ... it has the effect of unction upon the soul." The poem thus achieves on narrower grounds what had taken Lowell 140 lines to achieve in "The Quaker Graveyard in Nantucket." But unlike that poem, it does not present the vision which the experience earns. It ends where "Cistercians in Germany" ends, precisely at the moment when the union of man and God is to occur.

"Colloquy in Black Rock" likewise succeeds in reaching that new covenant which Lowell proposes in "The Quaker Graveyard in Nantucket." The opening stanza describes the body going into religious ecstasy. Its frenzy, like the beating of a drum, is the contemplative's preparation for the mystical bedchamber. This chamber, once entered, will lead, as the title implies, into a kind of religious colloquy which typifies a state of religious ecstasy and which terminates some contemplative acts.

The imagery of the poem is from St. Paul, with echoes of St.

Bonaventure and St. Bernard. A convert like Lowell, St. Paul writes in I Corinthians (13:1): "If I should speak with the tongues of men and angels, but do not have charity, I have become as sounding brass or a tinkling cymbal." This charity, "doing good actively to the neighbour," is one of the requisites of St. Bonaventure for achieving the active life after contemplation. It is the key to the poem. Again, it is St. Paul who, like the mystical bride in the Song of Songs, claims to be black and of whom St. Bernard writes, "Yet is it not he who was caught up into Paradise, who passing through the first and second heaven, attained, because of his purity, even to the third? ... This soul do you call black?" Finally, in Acts, is described the martyrdom of St. Stephen, who, in the poem, provides the link between the past and present.

"Footloose," heart beating faster, the contemplative of the poem sees modern Black Rock, Connecticut, turn into the "detritus of death," Black Mud, where Hungarian workmen give their life's blood to "martyre Stephen," the first of the Christian martyrs. As he was stoned, they are being destroyed by Mammon industrialism. His belief that God was to be found not only in the Judaic Temple but everywhere, helps them, however, toward their salvation, which, as the words "black mud" suggest to the contemplative, lies in overcoming the symbolic "Slough of Despond." The suggestion kindles him to a heightened intensity, conjuring this slough of self-pity in the images of the world about him. One of the necessary obstacles to the Celestial City of God, the slough must be realized and overcome if the penitent wishes to achieve salvation.

"Black mud" also recalls Nathaniel Hawthorne's description of the Concord River in "The Old Manse" and Lowell's subsequent use of the river to represent the forces which oppress modern man and which he must overcome:

> It is a marvel whence this perfect flower derives its loveliness and perfume, springing as it does from the black mud over which the river sleeps, and where lurk the slimy eel and speckled frog and the mud turtle, whom continual washing cannot cleanse. It is the very same black mud out of which the yellow lily sucks its obscene life and noisome odor. Thus we see, too, in the world that some persons assimilate only what is ugly and evil from the same moral circumstances which

supply good and beautiful results—the fragrance of celestial flowers—to the daily life of others.

The heightened pitch culminates in the last stanza with the re-alization of Christ walking on the black water. The image, the same one used in "The Drunken Fisherman," "In Memory of Arthur Winslow," "The Slough of Despond," and "Mary Winslow," sug-gests the Man-fisher nature of Christ's quest and the success of the contemplative. This is made more explicit in the close of the poem. In imagery which recalls Gerard Manley Hopkins' poem "Wind-hover," the poet is transformed into the "blue kingfisher." In this form, enkindled with God's love, he goes to meet that Host Who will suspend the frenzied world about him.

Achieving the union of God and man, as in "Cistercians in Germany" and "The North Sea Undertaker's Complaint," the poem neglects the knowledge which the contemplative learns. It stops precisely at the climax of the bedchamber where the poem should be opening into the new Truth. It seems to make union with God the end rather than the means of Truth and displays none of the peace and understanding and resolution which Lowell attains in "The Quaker Graveyard in Nantucket" and "In Mem-ory of Arthur Winslow." The poem ends merely in a brilliant flash of fire.

"Mary Winslow" takes Lowell's contemplative vision out of the current war setting and returns it to the personal family experi-ences of "In Memory of Arthur Winslow." Opening with a pic-ture of the Winslow descendants surrounding the dying woman, the poem portrays the salvation of Mary Winslow as in the manner she lived, keeping her house in order. In this portrait, the Charles River, longshoreman Charon, the shells of the Boston Boat Club, and finally the chapel bells recur. Their functions are identical with their uses in "Death from Cancer." They work to fetch Mary Winslow from her world of "childish bibelots."

Her death differs from her husband's in that hers is related to her original childish temperament and her illness. Throughout her life she has avoided both the Cain and Faust pitfalls of *Land of Un-likeness*, mainly through the childishness of her mind. Her illness has heightened this childishness, rendering her mind a *tabula rasa* and thereby aiding in her salvation. Through her childish inno-cence she has escaped to God. Her ecstasy, as rich as her husband's, is signaled in the last lines: "The bells cry: 'Come, / Come home,' the babbling Chapel belfry cries: / 'Come, Mary Winslow, come; I bell thee home.' "

This then is the extent and direction of Lowell's newly developed contemplative poems and provides much of the basic difference in the poet's view of the world as expressed in *Land of Unlikeness* and his views in *Lord Weary's Castle,* his second volume. He has merged the positions of art and religion into one aesthetic so that the two have become almost inextricably woven in the texture of his verse. At the same time, his view of salvation has become narrower. It is now more completely allied with the contemplative tradition and seems to consolidate into one step the various separate ways to salvation suggested in *Land of Unlikeness.* No longer can one augment baptismal likeness to God merely through a complete faith in Christ or an avoidance of war or a belief in the power of prayer or an ability to value worldly goods at no more than their price or by Catholicism. One must go beyond these means into the contemplative life.

CHAPTER FOUR

Lord Weary's Castle

Lord Weary's Castle (1946), in which Lowell first makes extensive use of his contemplative predilections, lets the reader know at the outset that it is in part a continuation of the ideas and techniques present in *Land of Unlikeness*. The sketch on the title page depicts the murder of Abel, and the title for the volume derives from a Scottish ballad in which injustice leads to blood and eventually to more blood for retribution. Much of the book continues the meditational tradition: The experiences continue to be objectified by relating them to epic events of the past or of literature, and the vision remains that of an Old Testament prophet in ungodly times. The major figures of St. Bernard, Christian Pilgrim, Faust, and Cain recur, and the major themes of mysticism, war, materialism, man's unlikeness to God, and man's salvation are repeated. New impetuses are suggested in such poems as "Charles the Fifth and the Peasant," "The Fens," "Buttercups," and "The First Sunday in Lent," but generally, the tone remains expository, didactic and critical.

The opening poem, "The Exile's Return," indicates that the volume's main concern is the world recovering from the war. It pictures the occupation of Germany as a parallel of Dante's famous descent into Hell. Yet, as in the poems of *Land of Unlikeness*, this Hell contains symbols of the country's return to Christianity— "already lily-stands / Burgeon the risen Rhineland, and a rough / Cathedral lifts its eye." It is the "Exile's" return, the epical echo of the return of the faithful from their Babylonian captivity. Told in imagery borrowed from Kröger's dream return to Lübeck in Thomas Mann's "Tonio Kröger," both this and the second poem of the volume, aptly called "The Holy Innocents," manifest the sublime faith of the earlier "Leviathan" that God will provide a new means for the remission of sins.

But soon the reader is back in the bleak war world of Cain and *Land of Unlikeness.* "Christmas Eve Under Hooker's Statue," "In Memory of Arthur Winslow," "Salem," "Concord," "Children of Light," "The Drunken Fisherman," "Napoleon Crosses the Berezina," "The Crucifix," "Dea Roma," and "The Slough of Despond" are reprinted from the earlier volume. A new sonnet, "France," portrays a view of the world war from the Crucifix, with Christ again the image of brotherhood. The opening line is a translation of the opening line of François Villon's "Epitaph," and the setting as well as other words and phrases owe much to Villon's poem. In such a world where Christ and Abel together hang forgotten on the gibbet, Lowell can only call in vain for love and understanding. It seems that with such an initial vision, the purgatorial trek up St. Peter's hill he describes in "The Holy Innocents" is doomed to failure.

Nevertheless, whereas frequently the poems in *Land of Unlikeness* did not altogether succeed in merging meditation and poetry, many of the later poems do. "At the Indian Killer's Grave," for example, despite its bleak outlook, becomes the newest, most ambitious, and most successful treatment of Lowell's Cain-Abel theme. Composed in part of segments from "The Park Street Cemetery" and "Cistercians in Germany," it returns the reader to the accusations of "Children of Light" and the indictments of John Easton. Added now is a description of King Philip's death at Mount Hope Neck, based on a letter by Richard Hutchinson: "This seasonable Prey was soon divided, they cut off his Head and Hands, and conveyed them to Rhode-Island, and quartered his Body, and hung it upon four Trees." A quotation from Nathaniel Hawthorne's story, "The Grey Champion," forms its inscription: "Here, also, are the veterans of King Philip's War, who burned villages and slaughtered young and old, with pious fierceness, while the godly souls throughout the land were helping them with prayer."

Like Hawthorne, Lowell is considering his Cain-Abel analogy in light of the end of an era during which the godly souls of our land were helping win World War II with prayer while young and old were being slaughtered. Coined especially for the new poem, the openings lines form an indictment against the "godly souls" of the Hawthorne story (and by analogy of our own day), whom history held in honor but subsequently forgot. Lowell wonders if at the Last Judgment they, too, will be so honored, or if their crimes, personified by King Philip's noose, will eventually hang them. In this speculation Jehoshaphat serves a dual purpose, being both the name of the valley of God's Last Judgment and of a ruler of Judah whose son Jocam murdered his brothers to gain control of the kingdom. As a reference to the book of Joel it stresses the moral nature of Lowell's vision; as an Adam figure it suggests the archetypal patterning of history.

Lapsing into the underworld descent of "The Park Street Cemetery," the poem continues with a description of modern Boston and the changes that have occurred since the deaths of the "stern Colonial magistrates and wards / Of Charles the Second." The Irish "hold the golden Statehouse / For good and always," and those colonists among the "dusty leaves and the frizzled lilac" lie decayed amid the whir and whirl of life. Returning to its initial theme of justice, the poem repeats its original Cain accusation more concretely.

King Philip speaks to these dead, taunting them with the results of their efforts to found a new Canaan. His taunts parody the peace pictured in "On the Eve of the Feast of the Immaculate Conception, 1942," where "mankind's Mother" like another Nimrod "danced on Satan's head":

> "Surely, this people is but grass,"
> He whispers, "this will pass;
> But, Sirs, the trollop dances on your skulls
> And breaks the hollow noddle like an egg
> That thought the world an eggshell."

The trollop, too, recalls Pearl, Hawthorne's symbol of God's mercy in *The Scarlet Letter*, and her dance over these same graves: "She now skipped irreverently from one grave to another; until, coming to the broad, flat, armorial tombstone of a departed worthy,—perhaps of Isaac Johnson himself,—she began to dance upon it." "The Judgment is at hand," King Philip warns, and it is unremitting.

The remainder of the poem shifts to Lowell's engulfing contemplative interests. Repeating the Deucalion-Jason image of "Cistercians in Germany," it goes on to entreat John, Matthew, Luke, and Mark to "gospel" the poet to the contemplative garden. There Mary rather than Bernard will become the "ecstatic womb, / As through the trellis peers the sudden Bridegroom." In the end, the poem remains one step farther away from contemplative vision, for in the earlier poem, the monks went beyond the Gospel into the "bedchamber."

In stressing the need for contemplative Truth, the poem conveys the energy and single-mindedness with which Lowell pursues his new vision. Its use of previous writings suggests the maelstrom of his imagination and engenders the belief that despite his ranging far and wide into issues derived from readings or conversations, Lowell's work will continue within quite narrow limits. Ironically, except for a possible pun on Major Thomas Savage, the Indian killer of the title does not figure at all in the main directions of the poem, let alone in its quest for Truth. Resting in the same underworld of "The Park Street Cemetery," his soul like the souls of "Adams, Otis, Hancock, Mather, Revere, and Franklin's mother" is beyond reviving.

With this poem Lowell's references to Indians and King Philip's War cease, and he ends his Cain-Abel analogy, leaving to God and time the ultimate judgment of the extent of the State's crimes. Why, one might ask, the abandonment? Perhaps with the immediacy of world war gone, the immediacy of this theme also disappears. With the "Ship of State" no longer asking "Christ to walk on blood," no need exists to press Cain-Abel analogies since there are neither Cains nor Abels. Still his position calls for blood to beget blood, war to beget war, injustice to beget injustice, and the concept of man as a descendant of Cain remains a shadowy, uneasy force.

The other new, successful, time-possessed poems of the volume seek also by brimstone to restore a balance of contemplation and meditation. "To Peter Taylor on the Feast of the Epiphany," "The Dead in Europe," "As a Plane Tree by the Water," and "Where the Rainbow Ends" move beyond the themes of war, Cain, and mysticism to the themes of world destruction. Abandoning his belief that man can reform, Lowell maintains in these poems that only the world-ending Last Judgment described in St. John's Apocalypse may suffice to turn man from his present evil course.

Therefore, he resumes the admonishing voice of *Land of Unlikeness*, selecting his images from Ezekiel, Joel, and John.

An epistle to a former Kenyon classmate, fiction writer Peter Hillsman Taylor, "To Peter Taylor on the Feast of the Epiphany," once more presents the world at the brink of total destruction. The Epiphany, the day on which the Wise Men presented their gifts to the Christ Child, opposes man's present situation. Rather than love, fear prevails. This fear may prompt man's return to Christ as it now prompts his trying to overcome death with money and dare-devil feats until his "cash and somersaulting snare / Fear with its fingered stop-watch in mid-air." The stopwatch distinguishes "saved" and "damned." The "saved," because of their contemplative natures, exist out of time in the timelessness of their mystical likenesses to God. By such means they usually escape the damning Faust and Cain archetypes. The "damned," because of their worldly natures, are locked in the world's temporal step and cannot escape. As a result, they are themselves brought to destruction.

"The Dead in Europe" reveals more of the frightening effects of the Allied "total bombings" and of those beings caught in time's lockstep. Echoing the views of Vergil and the people of Melville's Bedford in regard to the fates of those dead who lie in unconsecrated places, Lowell senses that those killed by the fire of bombs may have difficulty in crossing the Acheron to salvation. First implied in the exacting nature of the ferryboat ride in "Death from Cancer" and accented later by the sailing dead of "The Quaker Graveyard in Nantucket," these fears lie in the bombing described in the opening stanza:

> *After the planes unloaded, we fell down*
> *Buried together, unmarried men and women;*
> *Not crown of thorns, not iron, not Lombard crown,*
> *Not grilled and spindle spires pointing to heaven*
> *Could save us. Raise us, Mother, we fell down*
> *Here hugger-mugger in the jellied fire:*
> *Our sacred earth in our day was our curse.*

The dead have fallen into unconsecrated ground without the tribute paid them. Neither Christ, nor force, nor art, nor money can save them. The images and close texture recall the second and third sections of "In Memory of Arthur Winslow," in which the Pilgrim Makers pointed their steeples "lest the Word be dumb."

The second stanza offers a colloquy different from the one which ended "In Memory of Arthur Winslow." Rather than ask for a world-ending and world-saving flood, the voice entreats Mary to pray "For us whom the blockbusters marred and buried" and "When Satan scatters us on Rising-day" to "snatch our bodies from the fire." The last stanza pictures that great "Rising-day" as it appears in Apocalypse with the trumpets sounding at the four corners of the earth, causing the bones of the dead to tremble and reverberate. Mary is entreated again to "marry earth, sea, air and fire" and save these souls from damnation. Their fates, contained in the poem's refrain, are already sealed: "Our sacred earth in our day is our curse." Their lives were too earth-centered, too Mammon-materialistic; they were caught up and cursed by a damnation of their own making. The Allied position, little different from that of the Indian killer in "At the Indian Killer's Grave," suggests the reason for that damnation. Once again man will eventually have to atone for the murder of these dead in war.

In each of these poems the nature of man is contemporary, passive, and ambiguous. In "To Peter Taylor on the Feast of the Epiphany," man is the "hero skating on thin ice." In "The Dead in Europe," he is merely an unidentified "we." In both cases, he is universal and much different from the active Cain and Faust archetypes of *Land of Unlikeness*, for here man has lost his definitely assigned role. He can be anyone.

"As a Plane Tree by the Water" describes his society. Its title derives from Ecclesiasticus (24:19): "As a plane tree by the water in the streets, I was exalted." There the exaltation is of the contemplative after his mystical experience. Here "Darkness has called to darkness," suggesting an opposite view. The darkness seems in part taken from Psalms (43:18–21), where David describes man's state in God's covenant: "All this has come upon us, though we have not forgotten you, nor have we been disloyal to your covenant ... though you thrust us down into a place of misery and covered us over with darkness." It also seems to derive from the ninth plague of Exodus (10:21–22): "And the Lord said ...: Stretch out thy hand towards heaven: and may there be darkness upon the land of Egypt ... and Moses stretched forth his hand towards heaven: and there came a horrible darkness in all the land of Egypt for three days." Likewise the poem's refrain seems to derive from the fourth plague of Exodus (8:20–21): "Thus said the

Lord: Let my people go to sacrifice to me. But if thou wilt not let them go, behold I will send in upon thee, and upon thy servants, and upon thy houses all kinds of flies." These echoes and the poem's picture of "Babel-Boston" thus reverse the title, for darkness bespeaks a knowledge of evil, and in a land like ancient Babel wicked pride brings God's curse. The confusion of tongues is rampant.

Money is again the besetting evil as the Egyptian and Babylonian exiles are combined with man's current self-imposed exile from God. The poem indicates that the new world is a modern Babylon, a land of preparation for God, filled with the images of the Blessed Mother of God. As Walsingham had its Lady's shrine, so, too, Babylonian Boston has its Mary, "Our Lady of Babylon." Once the city was the apple of her eye. Now it is crusted with flies. As in Exodus, these flies symbolize God's intent that the people be released to worship Him. Thus, the signs of destruction are in full force. The sea walls of the poem become the cursed walls of Jericho, whose building caused Hiel, another Adam figure, to lose his sons (3 Kings 16:34), and the streets sing for the exodus, the world-ending flood of "A Prayer for My Grandfather to Our Lady" to set the people free to enter the contemplative life of the new covenant with God, where "all the world shall come to Walsingham."

Similarly, "Where the Rainbow Ends" suggests by its title that it is an extension of the contemplative direction begun in "In Memory of Arthur Winslow." The title, too, is ironic. The rainbow image of "The Quaker Graveyard in Nantucket" suggests a willful renewal of God's hopeful covenant with man now that World War II has ended. Here, in a vision, the poet sees Boston as the end of the rainbow: "I saw the sky descending, black and white, / Not blue, on Boston." The vision parallels St. John's in Apocalypse 21:2: "And I saw the holy city, New Jerusalem, coming down out of heaven from God, made ready as a bride adorned for her husband." But, as the reader soon learns, Boston exists outside the rainbow of God's will.

The deadwood at the foot of Ararat, where God made His covenant with Noah by sending him a rainbow, is being eaten by worms. Time and Death move upon the "thorn tree" of breath, symbolic of Christ. Time, as the second stanza makes explicit, is again damnation; it is the "serpent-Time, the rainbow's epitaph." The "serpent" is the Uroboros, the life-time serpent of medieval magic, as well as Satan. Caught up in time, the modern hero becomes an echo of his "damned" archetypal predecessor. Lowell, the prophet, describes himself as "a red arrow on this graph / Of Revelations," pointing the direction of mankind. As "Boston serpents whistle at the cold," he is at the high altar kneeling, asking for the wisdom implied, but not gained in "As a Plane Tree by the Water." The war has ended. "The dove has brought an olive branch to eat." Paralleling the action of Noah's dove in bringing the news of the new world, it is the Holy Ghost indicating to man that the olive branch of eternal peace is the direction of his salvation.

The poem's epithets for cold symbolize constriction and narrowness, greed and selfishness, Satan and evil. There is little hope for salvation except for the mystic who can achieve the mystical marriage of man and God and so escape:

> *The victim climbs the altar steps and sings:*
> *"Hosannah to the lion, lamb, and beast*
> *Who fans the furnace-face of IS with wings:*
> *I breathe the ether of my marriage feast."*

Thus, in spite of the "olive branch," the world has grown narrower by the two years of war separating the publication of the two volumes, and, in Lowell's mind, mankind's salvation has been made more difficult. This poem, the last one in the volume, ends the panoramic view begun in *Land of Unlikeness* on a pessimistic note. Not all men can be saved. Only those capable of achieving anagogic Truth can escape their Cain archetypes into salvation. These, as St. Bernard notes, are few compared to those who can live actively as Marthas and Lazaruses. They have been made even fewer, according to Lowell, by the materialism about them which minimizes their ability to contemplate. This materialism, in all of its aspects, gnaws most deeply at man's soul and prevents him from achieving the mystical experience he needs for salvation. The modern world, as a result, has become a Babel or a Vanity Fair avoiding God's worship in folly, and only destruction can save its inhabitants. Unless one accepts the implications of Walsingham that everyone is potentially a mystic, one wonders where the hope expressed in "Leviathan" has gone, the hope that God would send His saving Grace to man.

Each of these poems is based on war, and the war experience has ended. Lowell needs new impetuses to sustain him if he is to continue as a peacetime poet. The direction of these impetuses is indicated in such poems as "Charles the Fifth and the Peasant," "The Fens," "Buttercups," and "The First Sunday in Lent." Like the bulk of the war poems, they are pessimistic in outlook; however, none is overtly contemplative.

"Charles the Fifth and the Peasant" is one of five translations in the volume. It is patterned after a sonnet by Paul Valéry and weaves a richly colored tapestry in which are pictured the Emperor Charles V and a peasant. Its importance rests in showing what Lowell can do with scene. Its vivid description offers an excellent example of what he later, in a review, finds missing in A. E. Watts's translation of the Calydonian boar episode of Ovid's *Metamorphoses:* "These lines are like tapestry; they should have been tapestry. They should have been done into strangely spelt French. Their irregular and indistinct letters should have been deciphered one by one, as they unwound like a dragon on some tapestry huntsman's tapestry banner." Here with pinpoint observations Lowell creates a graphic impression akin to that of Titian's equestrian portrait of the emperor. His placing of "Titian" before "sunset" and "leg-of-mutton" before "beard" indicates his deliberate blending of his sources and suggests the kind of comparisons one may be expected to draw. The digression in lines 5–8 from the figure of Charles to what he stood for is patterned after a pictorial rather than a verbal irony. It could only be made if the action were still such that the viewer could attach sympathetic qualities to its subject. The fir trees of the poem are "disgruntled." The peasant becomes matter-of-fact. As such, the poem varies the meditational principle of making the reader an observer of the event, for here the event is a painting, rather than an actual canter into a German countryside.

Thematically, the poem continues Lowell's picture of man's broken covenant with God. In the last line the Ark, which had previously saved Noah, drowns in the deluge of Protestantism, the wolfhound biting at the emperor's spurs. The effect of Martin Luther's break with Catholicism is sweeping across Europe. Protestantism, as *Land of Unlikeness* establishes, relates to Mammon-materialism, the world's current ill. Catholicism, on the other hand, is the dock from which the saved souls depart and the waters on which the Fisherman walks. Without it man is lost.

"The Fens" represents a similar direction of Lowell's, also being derivative in origin. Describing the fens, a section of England which was confiscated by Henry VIII from the Catholic monasteries during the English Reformation, it relies heavily on the vituperative pen of social-reformer William Cobbett for its power. Here as in the case of "Our Lady of Walsingham," Lowell converts the prose of another writer into verse. Thus the following paragraph from *Rural Rides* provides the basic content:

> To Crowland, I went, as before stated, from Wisbeach, staying two nights at St. Edmund's. Here I was in the heart of the Fens. The whole country as *level* as the table on which I am now writing. The horizon like the sea in a dead calm: you see the morning sun come up, just as at sea; and see it go down over the rim, in just the same way as at sea in a calm. The land covered with beautiful grass, with sheep lying about upon it, as fat as hogs stretched out sleeping in a stye.... Every thing grows well here: earth without a stone so big as a pin's head; grass as thick as it can grow on the ground; immense bowling-greens separated by ditches; and not the sign of a dock or thistle or weed to be seen.... *Here* the grasping system takes *all* away....

To it are added the landlord, John Lord Russell, into whose hands Henry VIII entrusted the lands, and Lowell's own religious view. The "parochial" sunset "chilling the world to its four corners" is the loss of Catholicism hastening the world's end. The Lord High Sheriff settling as on a sea is God. The Bell now being borne away from the lands by the worldly sheriff is the "Bell" of "Mary Winslow," the symbol of resurrection; it once belonged to the monasteries. The line is an echo of the English ballad, "The Baily Beareth the Bell Away."

Similarly, additions of "Maundy Thursday" with its ritual of the Last Supper and of "Champs de Mars," where on July 14th Louis XVI swore to maintain the new constitution imposed upon him by the revolutionists, turn "1790" into a treatise on the opposition of Christianity and war. Otherwise, the poem derives from this passage in *The Memoirs of Baron Thiébault*:

> About six in the morning two of my comrades and I, in our forage caps, went out by the centre gate to

walk round the terraces, and get a breath of air. As we drew near the terrace on the rivers-side, the King [Louis XVI] came out of the small gate near the Pavilion of Flora, accompanied only by two gentlemen. Taking off our caps, we stood respectfully to let them pass; but seeing no reason to change our own route, we followed them at a distance of fifty or sixty paces. Having gone down and up the two horse-shoe flights of steps, he ... reached ... the Place Vendome.... Just then a lady came through the gate. She had a pretty little spaniel with her, which, before she noticed it, ran close up to the King. Making a low courtesy, she called the dog back in haste, but as the animal turned to run to its mistress, the King, who had a large cane in his hand, broke its back with a blow of his cudgel. Then, ... the King, delighted with his exploit, continued his walk, slouching rather more than usual, and laughing like any lout of a peasant.

"Buttercups" takes up Conrad Aiken's suggestion that Lowell stress the personal and try some poems of a nonreligious sort. Originally, it was part of "The Quaker Graveyard in Nantucket," but was excluded from the final version of that poem. In it, the poet recalls his childhood when "brassy sailor coats" made him and his playmates look like "black-eyed susans." Then, too, a bitter lesson had to be learned, for "There were shod hoofs behind the horseplay." The poet learns this lesson after a falling out nets him "a levelled broom-pole butt" on his chin. He retreats into his attic where he can imagine himself Napoleon, but a "huge cobwebbed print of Waterloo" reminds him once again of the defeat. A "red dragoon" is cropping the "buttercup" from the Emperor's grenadier.

Along with the print, retreat from life seems to be a Winslow heritage. Lowell makes the retreat and its dichotomy of dream and reality integral to *Life Studies*, where he handles his family and where he resumes the combination of personal anecdote, irregular lines, and irregular stanzas. Here the jump from religious to nonreligious poems offers mainly respite from the warnings of world end.

The personal anecdote of "In the Cage" offers another nonwar indication of the later work. Dealing with Lowell's prison experiences, it relies upon a recurrent bird imagery rather than a mention of Adam to bind up the "yard-bird" impressions. In its aura of world end are introduced the colored "fairy" and other inmates who people "Memories of West Street and Lepke."

"The First Sunday in Lent" brings into action a more immediate event of Lowell's epical vision, the destruction of Troy. The failure of Laomedon to pay for the building of the impregnable walls of that city, like Lord Weary's failure to pay for the building of his castle, sows seeds of the destruction. The event enlarges Lowell's earlier use of Vergil and Ovid and provides him with a new archetypal figure, Aeneas. Like Noah, the figure represents the founder of a new society within God's covenant to coincide with the possible founding of a new society after World War II. Lowell returns to it in "Between the Porch and the Altar," "The Death of the Sheriff," and "Falling Asleep over the Aeneid."

The parallel between Troy and modern America is made obvious in the poem. Commemorating the end of the ten-year war, the people of Troy bring inside their impregnable walls the wooden horse and celebrate. In this celebration they seal their doom, for overcome with wine and self-confidence, they fall easy victims to the Greeks hidden inside the horse. The end of World War II, if America is not wise, will produce a similar overconfidence and defeat. If it does, God is asked to raise a new "unblemished Adam" to celebrate His nature by founding a new society as Aeneas left burning Troy to found the new city of Rome.

Part Two of the poem, "The Ferris Wheel," pictures the world as a Vanity Fair carnival with Christian, the townsman, being brought to tears at the sight of all the frivolous people oblivious to their self-destruction. The images of vanity are again used to scare the reader back into religious activity, hopefully by Easter, the end of Lent. If this fails, the vision of world destruction rather than world salvation will be realized. The "Lenten" reflections of the poem thereby prepare the reader for the larger "Easter" visions of Lowell's successful contemplative poems.

In brief then, the new sources of Lowell's time-possessed poems —translations, paraphrase-adaptations, nonreligious personal recollection, and the epical parallel of the *Aeneid*—replace the more restricted sources of *Land of Unlikeness* and alter the poet's view considerably from that contained in the earlier volume. There one encountered six principal means of regaining God's likeness, and the predominant psychic archetypes were both negative—Faust and Cain. Now the means of regaining likeness have been reduced to one, "Catholic mysticism," and the archetypes include, besides St. Bernard and Christian Pilgrim, two builders of civilizations—Noah and Aeneas. With them the land, so to speak, may begin to take on its "Catholic framework." The notional assent to vision has been replaced by a closer approximation to mystical vision.

CHAPTER FIVE

The Dramatic and Narrative Voices

In the closing pages of *Lord Weary's Castle*, beginning with such poems as "Between the Porch and the Altar" and "After the Surprising Conversions," a new direction in Lowell's poetry appears. The direction manifests his reading of Friedrich Nietzsche and relies frequently on the run-on couplet and monologue devices of Robert Browning. It examples a change from the epical to dramatic and narrative forms and carries beyond Lowell's next volume of poetry, *The Mills of the Kavanaughs* (1951), into parts of *Life Studies* (1959). The reasons behind the direction are indicated by Lowell in a review of Robert Penn Warren's *Brother to Dragons* (1953). Analyzing poetry since Baudelaire and discussing the Martha-Mary distinctions between prose and verse, he summarizes the main tendency of the period as "repoeticizing": "Under this dying-to-the-world discipline the stiffest and most matter of fact items were repoeticized—quotations from John of the Cross, usury, statistics, conversations and newspaper clippings." Despite this, he finds contemporary verse lacking in two essentials of poetry: "These amazing new poems could absorb everything—everything, that is, except plot and character, just those things long poems have usually relied upon." The new direction, then, may be seen as an attempt to expand the range of poetry so as to include both plot and character. But to do so successfully, Lowell must also increase his range of character and action beyond the limited mysticism demanded by his current means of salvation, for the number of variations possible on the figure of St. Bernard is very small.

For readers of Joyce, this change is quite expected and is the next logical step in the evolution of aesthetic forms set up in *Portrait*. The poet has merely committed himself more completely to the aesthetic form and life of his poems. "The dramatic form," as Joyce explains in his novel, "is reached when the vitality which has flowed and eddied round each person fills every person with such vital force that he or she assumes a proper and intangible esthetic life." Lowell's poetry at this time does seem to be of its own direction committed more and more to the vitality and credibility of its characters rather than to the force of its ideas. The ironies of "Mary Winslow," for example, can only be resolved in so far as Mary Winslow's character comes alive, and it is a credit to Lowell's ability that he can manage this while keeping at the distance of a third-person presentation.

Likewise, the change proceeds logically from the contemplative traditions of St. Ignatius and St. Bernard, which begin in contemplation and end with a complete absorption in the subjects contemplated. Friedrich Nietzsche, in defining the aesthetic phenomenon, acknowledges the connection: "Why does Homer describe much more vividly than all the other poets? Because he contemplates much more. . . . If a man merely has the faculty of seeing perpetual vitality around him, . . . he will be a poet. If he but feels the impulse to transform himself and to speak from out the bodies and souls of others, he will be a dramatist." Hence, the merely descriptive poems of *Land of Unlikeness*, vitalized by contemplation, seek a life of their own. This is what happens to "The Park Street Cemetery" when its images and meaning are put into the mouth of King Philip in "At the Indian Killer's Grave."

In many respects then this dramatic form should be a fuller realization of the contemplative direction which Lowell's poetry was taking and should evolve neatly out of his earlier techniques. Yet it does not. Only "The Death of the Sheriff" achieves any of the religious pretensions of the earlier contemplative poems. "Between the Porch and the Altar," "Mr. Edwards and the Spider," and "After the Surprising Conversions" remain essentially moral and historical. Part of the reason is that the contemplative encounter which Lowell sought earlier in his poems and which one would expect to permeate the various interpretative levels of these poems seems to be precisely and expectedly the element disintegrating or, rather, being modified. In its place is a growing worldly concern with psychic "escapes from time." Lowell tries to unite this concern with what Nietzsche defines as the basis of classical tragedy, the duality of the Apollonian and Dionysian drives, and with what Pick, Lynch, Eliot, and others find to be the main problem of religious poetry, the attraction to and withdrawal from sensuous images. Thus, in the poems, "form," the Apollonian drive, is associated with the serpent, time, and sensuous images, and "escape from form," the Dionysian drive, with mysticism, salvation, and the withdrawal from sensuous images. Lowell's attempts to make these concerns mutually interchangeable within his old aesthetic often forces him to abandon the religious intentions of his earlier poems, and in *Lord Weary's Castle* the effect is an uneasy compromise between the old and new.

"Between the Porch and the Altar," the first poem in the volume to develop plot, is an excellent example of the compromise. Its four episodes, told from three different points of view, focus on the history of a man caught up and destroyed by time, mainly because he cannot escape his surroundings into the timelessness of salvation. In it, the magical Uroboros—the coiled serpent representing the life-time cycle—merges with the traditional Satan-serpent to provide a morally and technically well-worked poem, akin in many ways to the other meditational poems of the volume.

In the first episode a third-person narrative entitled "Mother and Son," the poet or chorus relates, "Meeting his mother makes him lose ten years, / Or is it twenty?" The mother, her possessions, her traditions, her ancestors, represent the world that the hero, an Odysseus in the underworld, must uphold. Through them the poem's basic image is established: "Time," whose ears "listen to the swallowed serpent, wound / Into its bowels." Linked to it is the Apollonian world of dreams, serpents, self-knowledge, and sobriety, in which portraits of the hero's ancestors defy time and the forebears are deified by descendants who fear death. From these forebears the hero must ask forgiveness for his own deviations. Morally, however, such figures are ultimately emblematic of what watch chains, slavers, and Nietzsche's Midas represent to Lowell, the Mammon-materialism of the twentieth century. They are damned by "A little golden snake that mouths a hook."

Pivoting upon the Apollonian-Dionysian duality between the damned and the saved, the poem becomes a first-person monologue in its second scene, the "Adam and Eve" episode. The Odyssean hero of the previous section tells of an afternoon of self-forgetfulness he spends in Concord with his mistress, here called Eve. A statue of the "embattled" farmer, representing Apollonian culture, signals again the ability of certain individuals to transcend time: "The farmer sizzles on his shaft all day. / He is content and centuries away / From white-hot Concord, and he stands on guard." A quotation from Sophocles' *Oedipus Rex* and from Nietzsche's tale of Midas and Silenus reminds him of the Dionysian world of the spirit: "Never to have lived is best." The second best, a Dionysian knows, is to die quickly. This is made Eve's function: "Man tasted Eve with death." With her, the possibility of the satanic serpent and of sin recurs. This possibility increases when, at the close of the section, the white of the statue connects with "the white church that Irish exiles made / For Patrick" and Patrick's association with snakes is recalled. As he is famed for having rid Ireland of snakes, the narrator wonders if Patrick will scorch the "red dragon" (Apocalypse 12:3) of his nerves to death. Meanwhile, Eve, portrayed as carrying a market basket of baking apples, spills them accidentally but significantly into the lake, where the narrator's eyes catch "the whorish slither of a snake / That chokes a duckling." When he tries to kiss Eve, scales glitter on their bodies, and both turn into time-caught and satanic serpents, sharing as archetypal Adams and Eves in their dark unlikenesses. On the pedestal, the Apollonian world melts.

The third episode, "Katharine's Dream," establishes a second voice—Eve's. Like her lover, she cannot escape her surroundings or her father: "He whispers that he really doesn't care / If I am your kept woman all my life, / Or ruin your two children and your wife; / But my dishonor makes him drink." The reverse of her lover's, her world is rendered Dionysian by her father's drinking and Apollonian by her dreams and self-knowledge. In this self-knowledge she walks the snow of St. Patrick's yard, wanting to repent, trying to cry out "and ask God's pardon" for their sin, but she finds that without her lover she cannot be saved. She runs in circles searching, approximating in that dream state the coiled Uroboros, only to drop at the end unforgiven "Against a padlocked bulkhead in a yard / Where faces redden and the snow is hard."

The last episode, "At the Altar," returns to the Odyssean hero. The "altar" of the title is a nightclub. It is Christmas, and the gold which has damned the narrator's forefathers glitters its damnation on him: "I sit at a gold table with my girl." The Christmas-tree bulbs turn into Easter eggs in the light, signifying again for Lowell man's only means of salvation, the cycle of Christ's birth, death, and resurrection. Later, in his car, the narrator races through seven red lights, the seven deadly sins, after which his highway lies unpatrolled. As the poem closes, he sees his destination—his soul coiled like a Uroboros on a spit in Hell.

What the poem seems to say is that man to achieve salvation must not only defy time as he did earlier, but that to this defiance must be added an "escape from form," the Dionysian drive. Pathetic as they are, the characters have refused this final step out of time-form into spirit and are, as a result, damned. This escape is what Katharine fails to achieve in her episode and what "Adam" runs from in the final scene. Consequently, the joyous fulfillment of Christ's welcome which ended a poem like "Mary Winslow" is nowhere to be found.

As drama the poem succeeds only insofar as it shifts its points of view in the various episodes. These shifts are a notable change from the single voice of Lowell's previous episodic structures, for by them the poem reaches beyond the limited persona of the epical vision to the personages of drama. The poem has completed what Nietzsche puts down as his first dramatic principle: The poet has transformed himself and spoken from the bodies and souls of others. "Adam," despite any likenesses to Lowell, is still a fictional rather than a dramatized persona. In addition, the poem fulfills part of Joyce's requisite of "filling every person with such vital force that he or she assumes a proper and intangible esthetic life." In doing so, it has retained much of the symbolism, theme, and other structure of Lowell's earlier work, retaining as it does epic parallels, dragons, Concord, Adam, Eve, and Christ.

"Mr. Edwards and the Spider" and "After the Surprising Conversions," the next poems in the new form, are intended as poems of character rather than narration. The poet borrows the techniques of such modern biographers as Lytton Strachey and Virginia Woolf. Using the person's own writings to bring him to life, these biographers tended to emphasize particularly the psychological rather than the historical attitude of the individual, often "debunking" the myths and legends surrounding him. Their techniques, as T. S. Eliot comments in his essay "Shakespeare and the

Stoicism of Seneca," are open to question: "It seems to me that one of the chief reasons for questioning Mr. Strachey's Shakespeare, and Mr. Murry's, and Mr. Lewis's, is the remarkable resemblance which they bear to Mr. Strachey, and Mr. Murry, and Mr. Lewis respectively." The objection may well be extended to Lowell, who in both poems uses the writings of the eighteenth-century Puritan theologian and philosopher Jonathan Edwards.

"Mr. Edwards and the Spider" takes most of its imagery and phrasing from Edwards' essay "Of Insects" and the sermons, "Sinners in the Hands of an Angry God" and "The Future Punishment of the Wicked Unavoidable and Intolerable." To see how successful it is as characterization, one has merely to compare Lowell's lines with those of the original. The first stanza, for example, follows by ellipsis the essence of Edwards' essay "Of Insects":

> *I saw the spiders marching through the air,*
> *Swimming from tree to tree that mildewed day*
> *In later August when the hay*
> *Came creaking to the barn. But where*
> *The wind is westerly,*
> *Where gnarled November makes the spiders fly*
> *Into the apparition of the sky,*
> *They purpose nothing but their ease and die*
> *Urgently beating east to sunrise and the sea;*

The lines of the essay read simply:

> Of these last [spiders] every One knows . . . their marching in the air from tree to tree . . . in a Dewey morning toward the latter end of august. . . . Once [I] saw a very large spider to my surprise swimming in the air in this manner, and Others have assured me that they Often have seen spiders fly. . . .

> . . . here in newengland I have Observed that they never fly except when the wind is westerly and . . . when they were hastening Directly towards the sea . . . from the Middle of August to the Middle of October. . . .

The changes—"mildewed" for "dewey" and "they purpose nothing" for "they were hastening"—add world decay and determinism to the original.

With the exception of the black widow spider image, stanzas two and three take their meaning and imagery from "Sinners in the Hands of an Angry God." After asking "What are we in the hands of the Great God?" the poet presents examples of the various attempts of what Edwards describes as "All wicked men's pains and *contrivance* . . . to escape hell, while they continue to reject Christ, and so remain wicked men." The thorns of stanza two seem to be from the Isaiah quotation Edwards uses in his sermon: "And the people shall be as the burnings of lime, as thorns cut up shall they be burnt in the fire." After examining these attempts, Lowell emerges in the closing lines of stanza three with a paraphrase of the famous: "The God that holds you over the pit of hell, much as one holds a spider, . . . looks upon you as worthy of nothing else, but to be cast into the fire."

> *It's well*
> *If God who holds you to the pit of hell,*
> *Much as one holds a spider, will destroy,*
> *Baffle and dissipate your soul.*

Likewise, stanzas four and five are based on the following lines from "The Future Punishment of the Wicked Unavoidable and Intolerable":

> You have often seen a spider . . . when thrown into the midst of a fierce flame, and have observed how immediately it yields to the force of the flames. There is no long struggle, no fighting against the fire, no strength exerted to oppose the heat, or to fly from it; but it immediately stretches forth itself and yields; . . . Here is a little image of what you will be the subjects of in hell. . ., the first moment you shall be cast into hell, all your strength will sink and be utterly abolished.

> . . . we cannot conceive what that sinking of the soul in such a case is. But to help your conception, imagine yourself to be cast . . . into the midst of a brick-kiln. . . . Imagine also that your body were to lie there . . . full of fire, as full within and without as a bright coal of fire. . . . If it were to be measured by a glass, how long would the glass seem to be running!

And after you had endured it for one minute, how overbearing would it be ... if you knew ... that after millions of millions of ages, your torment would be no nearer to an end. ... This is the death threatened in the law.

Converted into stanzaic form, these lines carry the brunt of Lowell's and also Edwards' message—the death of the soul by its opposition to the likeness of God:

> ... *I saw the spider die*
> *When thrown into the bowels of fierce fire:*
> *There's no long struggle, no desire*
> *To get up on its feet and fly—*
> *It stretches out its feet*
> *And dies. This is the sinner's last retreat;*
> *Yes, and no strength exerted on the heat*
> *Then sinews the abolished will, when sick*
> *And full of burning, it will whistle on a brick.*
>
> *But who can plumb the sinking of that soul?*
> *Josiah Hawley, picture yourself cast*
> *Into a brick-kiln where the blast*
> *Fans your quick vitals to a coal—*
> *If measured by a glass,*
> *How long would it seem burning! Let there pass*
> *A minute, ten, ten trillion; but the blaze*
> *Is infinite, eternal: this is death,*
> *To die and know it. This is the Black Widow, death.*

Through the use of the image on the black widow's abdomen—the hour-glass—the poem again adds an element of time to death. This time, Josiah Hawley, Edwards' uncle, who is to commit suicide in "After the Surprising Conversions," is caught in its lockstep and as a result is damned. It is interesting to note that this suicide occurred several years before the writing of these sermons. It seems doubtful, however, that Lowell, as one critic has suggested, is trying to make Edwards responsible for Hawley's death.

"After the Surprising Conversions" is, as Giovanni Giovannini pointed out in *The Explicator* (1951), "a close rendering, in many places a word-for-word copy, of a passage at the end of Jonathan

Edwards' *A Faithful Narrative of the Surprising Work of God in the Conversion of Many Hundred Souls* (1737), better known as *Narrative of Surprising Conversions....*" The passage, with the comparable lines of the poem in parenthesis, is quoted in its entirety:

In the latter part of May, it began to be very sensible (2–4) that the Spirit of God was gradually withdrawing from us (37–38), and after this Time Satan seemed to be more let loose (32), and raged in a dreadful manner. The first instance wherein it appear'd, was a Person's putting an end to his own Life, by cutting his Throat (29). He was a Gentleman of more than common Understanding (4–5), of strict Morals (5–6), religious in his Behaviour (6), and an useful honourable Person in the Town (8); but was of a Family that are exceeding prone to the Disease of Melancholy (9–10), and his Mother was killed with it (11). He had, from the beginning of this extraordinary time, been exceedingly concern'd about the State of his Soul (14), and there were some Things in his Experience, that appeared very hopefully (14–15); but he durst entertain no Hope concerning his own good Estate (20–22). Toward the latter part of his Time, he grew discouraged, and Melancholy grew amain upon him, till he was wholly overpower'd by it, and was in a great measure past a Capacity of receiving Advice, or being reasoned with to any purpose (26): The Devil took the advantage, and drove him into despairing Thoughts. He was kept awake a-nights, meditating Terror (25); And it was observed at last, that he was scarcely well capable of managing his ordinary Business, and was judged delirious by the Coroner's Inquest (29–30). The News of this extraordinarily affected the Minds of People here, and struck them as it were with Astonishment. After this, Multitudes in this, and other Towns, seemed to have it strongly suggested to 'em, and pressed upon 'em, to do as this Person had done (33–35). And many that seemed to be under no Melancholy, some pious Persons, that had no special Darkness, or Doubts about the goodness of their State (39), nor were under special Trouble or Concern or Mind about anything Spiritual or Temporal (40), yet had it urged upon 'em, as if somebody had spoken to 'em, *Cut your own Throat, now is a good Opportunity*. Now; now!

The poem, again with its emphasis on time—in this instance through its addition of "September twenty-second," pictures man against the timeless cycle of nature. The purpose of this picture is to show that living does not end with one's dying, or even with the deaths of many, but is a continuous cycle as the poem's paradisical "apples" and redemptive "small-mouth bass." The date, September 22, is important on two counts: It is the feast day of St. Thomas of Villanova, who sent the first Augustinians to the Americas as missionaries, and like Edwards' sermons, those of St. Thomas "were followed by a wonderful change in the lives of men in all places he visited." Now at this later date, when Christianity is leaving America and when Edwards' sermons produce several suicides instead of conversions, the juxtaposition provides an irony of a sort similar to and yet the complete reverse of that in "Death from Cancer," in which Arthur Winslow dies on Easter, the day symbolizing resurrection. Here the forces that would bring life cause death instead.

September 22 is also the date of the death of Persephone. It is the beginning of fall, which Lowell equates in both "The Mills of the Kavanaughs" and "David to Bathsheba" with man's Fall: "Perhaps it took / Of fall, the Fall?" It is the date on which man must move out of the calendar year in order to achieve his salvation. At the beginning of the poem, the date is opposed to "our Lord's Ascension," and at the end to "apples" and "fish," two traditional emblems for Christ.

Other changes reflect Lowell's earlier-mentioned dislike of capitalism. Edwards' unidentified "somebody" is changed into a "peddler." The addition of a sermon "on a text from Kings," most likely "The Unreasonableness of Indetermination in Religion," based upon 1 Kings (18:21), reemphasizes this point. The text reads: "And Elijah came unto all the people, and said, How long halt ye between two opinions? If the Lord be God, follow him; but if Baal, then follow him. And the people answered him not a word." In the sermon Edwards, like Lowell, points out: "There are but two masters, to one of which we must be reputed the servants, Baal and Jehovah, God and Mammon: There are but two competitors for the possession of us, Christ and the devil." Many "spend away their lives without making their choice, putting that off, though they do in the mean time practically choose the service of Satan." Thus, with the addition of time-life cycles to both "Mr. Edwards and the Spider" and "After the Surprising Conversions," and the addition of economics to the second poem, Lowell has insinuated himself into the character of Jonathan Edwards. He further insinuates himself into Edwards' character by changing the source of Hawley's melancholy. It is no longer parental and hereditary. This change makes the act of suicide volitional and, to this extent places perhaps more of the responsibility for it on Edwards' Calvinistic sermons. Moreover, the shift in Hawley's character from "honorable" (worthy of honor) to "honored" (respected) heightens the effect of the act.

As each of these poems is concerned primarily with man's unlikeness to God, each avoids the contemplative structure of colloquy, despite an ineffectual symbolizing of potential likeness which closes "After the Surprising Conversions." Yet the poems do succeed as poems and thus prepare for the equally noncontemplative and successful character poems, "Falling Asleep over the Aeneid" and "Ford Madox Ford." Their only fault—conceivable in Lowell's attempt to return plot and character to modern poetry—is in failing to achieve anything approximating plot. They are static character delineations.

The last of the poems in *Lord Weary's Castle* to offer any additional interest in plot and character is the two-part "The Death of the Sheriff." Like "Between the Porch and the Altar," the poem is Lowell's invention. It follows the actions of a man's incestuous lovemaking and the death of his sheriff cousin who has turned homicidally insane. Both actions are established means of escaping the life-time cycle and account for the poem's "Fall"-autumn images. The one attempt by the sheriff succeeds. Yet, both actions lead to a preponderance of garish situations which the poem, with its Elizabethan shifts in scene, fails finally to assimilate.

The sheriff's successful escape from time is shown when his corpse is taken by the undertaker "who collects antiques." The implication in the undertaker's interest is that the sheriff's salvation has been gained by going backward. This is made more explicit when his soul rises to Heaven on an archaic "wain," accompanied by Angels, presented in their Dantean, quasi-pagan forms of constellations. The actual means of the escape seem to be twofold: retribution for sin and lack of responsibility for future action. The second, naturally enough, stems from his eventual insanity. Viewed by the cousins, who are trying to break the lockstep of their existence by the perversion of their souls through the equally primitive means of incest, this escape opposes, during their lovemaking, their failure and their thought of atonement.

The second part of the poem reveals an Apollonian world similar to that in "The First Sunday in Lent." The hero, a modern Aeneas, recalls the ancient tale of Poseidon, Apollo, and Laomedon, in which the sea-god received no pay for his part in building Troy's impregnable walls. A toppling candelabrum illuminates an heirloom painting of Poseidon building the wall. The realization follows that man has not changed much since the founding of Rome. Traditionally associated with Apollo, Troy is further linked in the hero's mind with the Apollonian worship of ancestors, longevity, and form: "Now I can let my father, wife and son / Banquet Apollo for Laomedon." Against this worship, only "white Helen," the symbol of Troy's destruction and mankind's salvation through the founding of Rome, can save him. He awaits her and finds at the end that, unlike his cousin, he is committed to the things of this world, to death. Again this hero resembles Lowell's epical persona in likes, aims, and dislikes; but again he is a fictional, not a dramatized persona.

Tighter in structure than "Between the Porch and the Altar," the poem follows a simple chronology of events about the sheriff's burial. In this arrangement, the episodes assume a stronger sense of continuity and a surer sense of drama. Nonetheless, neither poem displays a particularly satisfying dramatic sense. Drama hinges on the conflict between two or more forces real or imagined, and in these poems Lowell misses the immediacy of such conflicts. The results are soliloquies and monologues cut off from the dramatic moments which inspire them. Consequently, he resorts to attracting the reader by substituting melodramatic incidents for tension. These, in turn, by their disproportion lessen the effectiveness of the dramatic statements.

Likewise, the moral level of "The Death of the Sheriff" causes the reader some concern, for it betrays a growing breach between salvation and "escape from time." The lovers who are doomed from the beginning by their incestuous actions derive little but awareness from the poet. With the wrath of a vengeful god, he seems to have created a world aware of life-time cycles, peopled it with a *genus durum*, and provided no real means by which to escape successfully. The sheriff, who escapes through insanity, offers the only clearly defined solution to the dilemma. However, this solution is bootless; all the world cannot go insane. Lowell must either find a new solution if his reformation of mankind is to succeed, or abandon this area of interest altogether if God's likeness has ceased to be his emphasis. Moreover, his hero seems to lack variety. Regardless of any original differences, being forced to serve a prescribed mystical and ecstatic structure imparts a sameness to his character which, in turn, added to the usual repetitiousness of Lowell's themes, produces a static, formulaic body of poetry. It is here, then, as well as in the concept of drama and the moral level, that, having expanded the character range of his poetry and having achieved some degree of plot, Lowell may need to strengthen his poems if he is to achieve again any of his successful, early mergings of poetry and Catholicism.

CHAPTER SIX

The Mills of the Kavanaughs

In *The Mills of the Kavanaughs* Lowell's interest in plot and character prompts seven new poems, all primarily human, time-possessed, and definite. Ranging into the "longer poem" category, they complete the disintegration of the anagogical level in Lowell's poetry and, at the same time, provide more diversification in his characterizations. The realization that his basic poetic vision relied heavily on sensuous detail, that he was unable to develop, as Dante had, a new way of looking at things, that his interest was in the active rather than the contemplative life, or that drama is basically anthropocentric rather than theocentric may account for this disintegration. In any case, the disintegration provides for the inclusion of new ideas and personages neither interested in nor capable of understanding the structure of religious contemplation. Having emerged, these voices receive a sympathy and understanding not often shown previously by the poet.

The only poems in the volume which in any way try to reverse this tendency and return to Lowell's earlier contemplative structure are "Falling Asleep over the Aeneid" and "Her Dead Brother." Both, however, in their choices of subject matter and theme merely reinforce the necessity of abandoning the form. "Falling Asleep over the Aeneid," a character poem, depicts the Lowell persona in an old man in Concord who "forgets to go to morning services. He falls asleep while reading Vergil, and dreams that he is Aeneas at the funeral of Pallas, an Italian prince." By his action, he is seeking, like the hero of "The Death of the Sheriff," to break the cycle of his existence, for he senses that he, too, must go backward to salvation. But rather than go insane, he tries to accomplish this escape through dreams. Religiously, this poem is by far the more successful of the two attempts.

Expressionistic in its distortion of the outer world and its violent dislocations of time and space, the poem images the world as it appears to the troubled mind of the hero. This world is pictured in a long interior monologue in which the hero is about to repeat in his dreams actions which immortalized his predecessor. As did "Mr. Edwards and the Spider," the poem borrows extensively from its source and presents the thoughts of the modern-day Aeneas in a paraphrase-translation from the *Aeneid*. For example, the lines, "And I stand up and heil the thousand men / Who carry Pallas," come from Book XI:

> *Haec ubi deflevit, tolli miserabile corpus*
> *imperat, et toto lectos ex agmine mittit*
> *mille viros. . . .*

In the same manner, later in the poem, the following lines from Book XI:

> *hic iuvenem agresti sublimen stramine ponunt*
> *qualem virgineo demessum pollice florem . . .*
> *cui neque fulgo adhuc nec dum sua forma recessit;*
> *non iam mater alit tellus virisques ministrat,*

are rendered:

> *You are the flower that country girls have caught,*
> *. . . the design*
> *Has not yet left it, and the petals shine;*
> *The earth, its mother, has, at last, no help. . . .*

Interposed between these borrowings are references to Book IV of the *Aeneid*, which predicts this tragedy, quotations from St. Francis de Sales's *Treatise on the Love of God*, and allusions to Nietzsche.

The whole poem, a love poem, depicts the various kinds of love possible on earth. It begins with Queen Dido's thwarted, all-consuming love. Against her famous curse, "First, let him see his friends in battle slain, / And their untimely fate lament in vain," it pictures a modern Aeneas repeating the farewell kiss of her sister:

"I greet the body, lip to lip." The perpetual war which Dido bequeathed Rome as a consequence of Aeneas' desertion has begun, and from it hopefully there may be the founding of a new Rome.

Lowell's poem then goes on to represent other kinds of love. His description of Aeneas covering the body demonstrates love for one's fellowman:

> But I take his pall,
> Stiff with its gold and purple, and recall
> How Dido hugged it to her, while she toiled,
> Laughing—her golden threads, a serpent coiled
> In cypress. Now I lay it like a sheet;
> It clinks and settles down upon his feet,
> The careless yellow hair that seemed to burn
> Beforehand.

Like the earlier passages, it is taken from Vergil:

> tum geminas vestis auroque ostroque regentis
> extulit Aeneas, quas illi laeta laborum
> ipsa suis quondam manibus Sidonia Dido
> fecerat et tenui telas discreverat auro.
> harum unam iuveni supremum maestus honorem
> induit arsurasque comas obnubit amictu. . . .

The memorable Aethon section echoes Achilles' death in the *Iliad* and extends this love to brute animals:

> Aethon, the hero's charger, and its ears
> Prick, and it steps and steps, and stately tears
> Lather its teeth; and then the harlots bring
> The hero's charms and baton—but the King,
> Vain-glorious Turnus, carried off the rest.

It, too, derives from Vergil:

> post bellator equus positis insignibus Aethon
> it lacrimans guttisque umectat grandibus ora.
> hastam alii galeamque ferunt; nam cetera Turnus
> victor habet.

But in this war two additional kinds of love are needed: St. Francis de Sales's love of God, especially in the bird-priest sequences, and Nietzsche's love of spirit as Lowell asks the speaker to "try, / O Child of Aphrodite, try to die: / To die is life." For both Nietzsche and St. Francis death is an escape from form, a release into eternal love. As St. Francis states: "... this soul, who, as a heavenly nightingale..., cannot at will sing the benediction of his eternal love, ... cries ... deliver poor me from the cage of my body, free me from this little prison...." This liberation is what is achieved when Pallas is compared to "A wild bee-pillaged honeysuckle brought / To the returning bridegroom." The metaphor, God being the Eternal Bridegroom, is one which St. Francis uses for the soul of the meditator: "In which our spirit... be filled, ... as a sacred bee, moves over the flowers of holy mysteries, to extract from them the honey of divine love." The implied religious ecstasy of the metaphor is the closest any figure gets to mysticism.

This discussion of love leads not to the founding of a new Rome but to the impending death of heroism, pictured in the closing lines of the poem when the modern Aeneas is awakened by the closing of the church services. The bells of the church have frightened away the yellowhammers who had droned him to sleep, and he is reminded now of his great aunt who used to scold him: "Vergil must keep the Sabbath." Her husband, his Uncle Charles, appears dressed in the bird-peaked uniform of the Civil War and frowned upon by visions of Philip Brooks and Grant. He has achieved salvation by giving his life for others. Thus, like the lovers in "The Death of the Sheriff," the hero has only become aware of his need for salvation and cannot achieve it, committed as he is to the Apollonian traditions of his family and the tenuous make-believe valor of dreams. In this sense the poem seems to differentiate between Uncle Charles, who gave his life to oppose slavery, and Vergil, who merely dreams of doing something heroic. Actions, not intentions, Lowell seems to say again, are the basis for salvation, and at the same time he indicates that the present is not capable of such saving actions.

A thematic collage of several previous poems, "Her Dead Brother" introduces a pair of troubled lovers and relates the causes of the suicide of the narrator after her brother's death in war. The first section outlines the nature of their life-time cycle and the religious symbols again at work—the Lion of St. Mark, the dragon, water, and ice. Paired as opposing life-death forces, they recur at intervals throughout the narrative. Once more incest—the most primitive means of opposing the Uroboros and the perversion of love, the nature of man's soul—forms the principal device of the characters' attempted escape.

The poem opens with the stock contemplative "storeroom" imagery of the Lion of St. Mark. This lion, crested in the windows of the house, opposes the coiled, German-silver picture frame of the brother's portrait, which mirrors the dragonish sunset. The images, taken from the Apocalypse, reflect the same world-ending Apollonian state which begins "Between the Porch and the Altar," where the time-bound "Adam" was shown rummaging through similar artifacts in his mother's home, recalling the fall of Troy. As in that poem, the description ends with references to Shakespeare and Homer that convey acceptance of a contradictory Dionysian spiritism: "All's well that ends: / Achilles dead is greater than the living." Achilles, who represents for the speaker both her brother and the Dionysian, awakens her to the emptiness and futility of her present ice-house state and urges her forward into escape.

In the "garden" imagery of the second stanza, the narrator recalls the "bird-watching" summer excursions with her brother to Sheepscot and the milk-snake which he killed and which her father shellacked to the ice-house door. Later, during the memory's move into winter, she recalls the August 23 of their sin—the anniversary of the Sacco-Vanzetti execution—when their mother and her maids motored to Stowe. These recollections shape and collide in her mind, beginning to take on strange meanings when she is interrupted by the sounds of her husband's Packard crunching up the drive. The effect of these collisions is again to turn the heroes into symbolic coiled serpents.

The remainder of the poem, with the suicidal delirium of its flowing gas, describes merely, as did the previous poem, the attempt to unwind these images and find an end to the life-time cycle: "The gas, uncoiling from my oven burners, dims / The face above this bottled *Water Witch.*" Occurring three months after the first episode, this part opens with the distraught sister envisioning the circumstances of her brother's death: "The ice is out: the tidal current swims / Its blocks against the launches as they pitch / Under the cruisers of my Brother's fleet." The "Water Witch," the name of a knockabout manned by her brother and fouled in Boston Light, presents to her, in its model and echo of the past, a vessel to bring both to afterlife. Its name, indicative of the romanticism of that past, derives from a novel by James Fenimore Cooper in which a pirate captain, known as "The Skimmer of the Seas," mans a small brigantine, "Water Witch." The captain abducts a beautiful heiress, Alinda de Barbarie, and is pursued by Alinda's suitor, Captain Ludlow. Finally, he restores Alinda to her suitor.

The poem's voyage into afterlife is more complicated and detailed than the already discarded swan-journey of "Death from Cancer." Through the earlier milk-snake image, it is linked in the sister's delirium with the ice-house. She and her brother must maneuver the yacht through the ice-flows of the harbor, where the ice, symbolizing the soul in its contained or Apollonian form, presents the main obstacle to safe passage. Heeling in the fog and being pushed by the covenant of her rainbow sail, the "Witch" pauses briefly as her winds turn mute. Then, reminiscent of "The Death of the Sheriff," the Lord appears dark, like the night with all its constellations, and the narrator goes into a frenzied ecstasy: "The Lord is dark, and holy is His name; / By my own hands, into His hands! My burners / Sing like a kettle." But quickly this ecstasy turns into hysteria when the launches she envisions come on to sink the cruisers of her brother's fleet, and the yacht dies. Afterward comes the final, quiet realization that she has not achieved the likeness of God, but the likeness of her dead brother.

The failure of both poems to achieve mystical visions results not from technique, since all the elements of the previous successful contemplative poems are present, but from the basic subject matter of the poems. In choosing the "old man in Concord" in "Falling Asleep over the Aeneid," Lowell has chosen a person interested, like Martha, in the active life, in worldly not contemplative love. Likewise, in choosing incest and suicide for the plot of "Her Dead Brother," he is forced again by the moral level of his poem to recondemn its hero. The sister, who feels that she is approaching the true Noonday, is actually enchanted by Hypocrisy, the noonday devil. The situation echoes the one described by St. Bernard in his sermons *On the Song of Songs* in his warning of the noonday devil who often comes disguised, sometimes even as the true Noonday: "The Apostles, also, on a certain occasion when they were laboring at the oars, with the wind against them tossing their little boat about, seeing the Lord walking upon the water and thinking it was an apparition, so that they cried out for fear—did they not betray a suspicion of the noonday devil?"

Thus, in the face of these changes in subject matter, Lowell's attempt to uphold his earlier contemplative structure results in a growing breach between style and subject matter which he tries to close by forcing his subject matter. His current concerns, reflecting those of his time-damned heroes, are not contemplative and metaphysical, but worldly and moral. Yet by dint of habit, he seems to avoid new structures which may be more appropriate to his needs. The failure of adjustment is most evident in the two plot and character poems and in the remaining poems of the volume which, as their subjects move farther from contemplation, show more clearly the separation. With their meditational structures, they come no closer to filling the gap.

Despite its title, "Mother Marie Therese," the next poem in the volume, returns to the noncontemplative meditational direction of Lowell's work. Its portrayal of a nun in the postcontemplative, active life of a Martha reveals one temporary solution. Time, the metaphysical villain of the six previously discussed poems, is absent, for as Father Turbot observes, "N-n-nothing is so d-dead / As a dead s-s-sister." Even the nun concludes one must "tarry a little" and "disregard Time's wings and armor." Traditionally dead to the world, she is wrapped in the eternal peace which most of Lowell's other characters seek. In this peace—"chastised" to the Rule's restraint, her "worldly serpent" washed by Christ's sweat—she has returned to the active life to await world end. But, as St. Bonaventure points out in his *Meditations on the Life of Christ*, it is the active life in its second stage—"in doing good actively to the neighbour . . . as in ruling, teaching, and helping in the salvation of souls." Thus in contrast to the heroes of "Between the Porch and the Altar" and "Her Dead Brother," she lives her life, pictured as the demanding "émigrée in this world and the next," without any compulsion to return to contemplation. In her, Lowell shows for the first time both the peace of the truly Christian life which his characters try to achieve and an acceptable means of attempting it.

Concerned with a second nun's recollection of that peace and of the Mother's steadying hand, the poem describes a time when nuns are becoming increasingly unsettled and the chances of leading a truly Christian life are becoming more remote. Although God's Providence has mastered them, even a "buck ruffed grouse" finds their "stern virginity / *Contra naturam*." Remembered for her "strangled grouse and snow-shoe rabbits," the Mother had been a stern master of unsettled novices before her drowning on an excursion in the Atlantic. Her firm, aristocratic ways, representative of the uncompromising Hohenzollern standards of her background, have disappeared, and the Order now neglects even to pay its occasional respects. Often not up to the exacting demands of its calling, it sees only a comparable neglect by the warring world outside, whose aims have become the Order's opposite, self-destruction rather than salvation: "Mother, we must give ground, / Little by little; but it does no good." The Mother, who refused to give ground in her lifetime, is being washed by the waters of the Atlantic for her final encounter with God.

A brilliant tribute to both the figure of Mother Marie Therese and her calling, the poem achieves not only a certain "worldliness," but approaches in its structure and content a degree of sympathy not previously common in Lowell's work. Of the two levels on which it exists, neither is at variance with the subject matter. The historical level compassionately pursues the qualities which made the Order strong, the snuffing of crones' and cretins' fear, and the moral level undertakes the actions of its four characters, including the Atlantic. Both function easily and without the poet's usual resort to nightmarish and melodramatic situation. Like "Falling Asleep over the Aeneid," they combine into an interior monologue which, rather than being expressionistic, imitates the stylized soliloquy of the Elizabethan stage. As a result, it comes closest of all the poems discussed to achieving the intended dramatic moment. In these accomplishments as well as in Lowell's new humanity and warmth, it well deserves Randall Jarrell's tag as "the best poem Mr. Lowell has ever written."

The poem which follows it, "David and Bathsheba in the Public Garden," tries to present a seventeenth-century dialogue of Body and Soul and fails on at least two grounds to equal the success of "Mother Marie Therese." Nevertheless, its attempt to develop plot and character through dialogue while maintaining some semblance of a single verse style does represent a change from Lowell's previous structures. Presenting the Boston counterparts of the Biblical lovers, the poem suggests an expansion of character by dealing with two actors. This requires character delineation and variety. As realized, however, the poem fails to provide this expansion. Both characters are extremely mannered and allusive and seem the manifestation of a single voice. As Randall Jarrell remarks, "They both . . .

talk just like Mr. Lowell." Likewise, the poem, a reiteration of Lowell's earlier presentments on man's unlikeness to God, fails in its meditational structure and suffers from the same lifelessness which marked his notional assents to vision in *Land of Unlikeness*.

Set at the start of the marriage, "David to Bathsheba" details the attempts to make Bathsheba forget her wronged husband Uriah and assume her role as David's wife. To the question "And he is nothing after death but ground, / Anger and anguish, David?" he replies that he must live according to the nature of his soul: "I lie / Drinking our likeness from the water. Look: / The Lion's mane and age! Surely, I will not die." But the question, already posed and answered to the poet's satisfaction in "At the Indian Killer's Grave," has an extremely clearcut and sinister solution: At the Last Judgment, those transgressed against will judge the souls of the transgressors. This is Bathsheba's fear and her eventual conviction as the poem moves into its second part, "Bathsheba's Lament in the Garden."

Years later David has taken a new wife, Abishag, and Bathsheba sits in the garden again, talking to her son. Her mind rambles over the past events, and she asks herself once more if Uriah will sit in judgment. Without David's assurance of Divine purpose, she is troubled by what her actions have brought about—the death of Uriah, David's new distance, and the wars which have set David against his sons and the sons against each other. Consistent with "At the Indian Killer's Grave," her conclusion—"I must surely die"—opposes David's optimistic statement and ends the poem.

"The Fat Man in the Mirror," which follows, is an extremely worldly and successful picture of a hair-bellied, dog-eyed, middle-aged man just awakening to the fact of his condition. Taken in part from Franz Werfel's "Der Dicke Mann im Spiegel," the poem shuns the quiet, sinister sentimentality of the original for the hustle-bustle bravado of remembered childhood. Free of its author's usual preoccupation with death and guilt, it is an extremely gay, melodic song whose success as dramatic form rests entirely in a direct, lyrical, and compassionate presentation. Its limitation is a lack of Lowell's usual "significant" content.

With the nightmare world of "Thanksgiving's Over," this content returns. The structure of the poem, a variation of the expressionistic structure of "Falling Asleep over the Aeneid," follows the dream of a man whose wife, "a German-American Catholic," leaped from the window of their apartment before her eventual death in a Vermont sanitorium. Concerned with the death of love in their marriage, the poem develops through a series of dialogues between the dead woman and her sleeping husband. The technique, first used in "David and Bathsheba in the Public Garden," is aided in this instance by several factors. The wife, presented as a figment of her husband's imagination, takes on the hallucinatory aspect of a mystical experience, and Lowell can employ devices of the contemplative structure without resorting to mysticism. In addition, so presented, she need not have the character differentiation of a separate person.

The opening lines of the poem establish the world outside the room, and the noises of New York City's "El" purposely echo those of the opening lines of "Falling Asleep over the Aeneid" with their mating yellowhammers. Here "warred" instead of "mating" and "night" instead of "sun" suggest the differences between the conditions of the poems. In this poem Christ, traditionally portrayed as "light" and "love," is missing, and the world is making little effort to recover Him. Bird imagery again conveys the nature of the Christian soul, but in non-Christian surroundings the soul is liberated by insanity not death. Insanity is identified in the poem with the parrot who "possesses" the wife and who represents by his name and action "imitation" or "likeness." He is equated in the demented wife's mind with the Lord: "The Lord is Brother Parrot, and a friend."

Knowing what such birds have done to her mind, her husband Michael asks "Whose friend?" and wakens to the El's rattle as a train passes. Noticing anew the barred windows and the various bird-representations throughout the apartment, he falls asleep again. In his sleep his wife returns to tell him that before he sent her off to Vermont he committed his greatest sin by destroying her capacity for love. For this he would be damned. Meanwhile, she, in her insane world of perpetual spring and birds, traces their idyllic youthful love to the autumn when "Flocks / Scavenge for El Dorado in the hemlocks." Protected in this world by Venus, the goddess of love, she opposes her husband, "Archangel Michael," and rapidly passes through a series of mentally warped Biblical and mythological love tales including that of Susannah and the Elders, until she finally arrives at the scene where her husband's lack of love causes her leap from the window. She describes her commitment, like the goddess Persephone's, as a winter and entreats her husband to resurrect her into spring through love. Fearing the dead as well as death, he awakens trembling from this dream and says a rosary to still their souls.

In its way, the poem opposes point for point the illustrations of love in "Falling Asleep over the Aeneid" and demonstrates by negative examples the world as it is without the understanding and humanity of one's fellowman. Love and religion are set in conflict and both suffer. Since love is the nature of the soul, the poem is one of the most horrifying that Lowell has written.

But if Lowell can exclude contemplation from the structure of his poems, he cannot exclude his interest in flights from form. "The Mills of the Kavanaughs," the last written poem of the volume and the longest that Lowell has yet published, represents his efforts to deal with the problem without returning to mysticism. A composite of techniques borrowed from poems discussed, it opens with a woman sitting in her garden with her Bible, "Sol," playing solitaire, and recollecting her life. With its "rut of weeds that serpents down a hill" and its Apollonian image of Persephone, the goddess of immortality, the life in the opening stanza suggests the recurrence of the problem which plagued many of Lowell's characters, the archetypal Uroboros. Against that suggestion Anne Kavanaugh, armed with "Sol" and dressed in dungarees, represents a new type of heroine to meet the situation. Her husband Harry, the namesake of a line of English kings and heir to the Kavanaugh tradition as well as protector and restorer of the Kavanaugh properties (an old family mansion in Damariscotta Mills, Maine), recalls the other heroes who have died opposing time. To them he adds the imaginary lover, the destructive guilts, the withdrawals, and at times even the description found in Jean Stafford's story of marital dissolution, "A Country Love Story," suggesting perhaps a common biographical incident from their marriage linking the story, this poem, and a later poem, "The Old Flame." This possibility is further strengthened by the Kavanaugh motto: "Cut down, we flourish." The motto is that of Lowell's maternal ancestors, the Winslows.

The history of the Kavanaugh tradition, currently being destroyed by time and taxes, is outlined in the second stanza. While playing cards Anne briefly traces the events which made her Mrs. Kavanaugh and placed her in this garden. Her first recollection is her first visit as a trespasser to the peaceful Kavanaugh world.

Then, too, she had "queened" it. Now, brought back to the present by the pool's statues, she admonishes her dead husband for having given up too quickly and is reminded in turn by "Sol" that her "gambling with herself / Is love of self." She thinks of Daphne, who was so in love with herself that she resisted the advances of the sun-god Apollo. "Sol," who represents in a way the new sun-god and her salvation, must not be so thwarted. Absorbed in these thoughts, she forgets that her husband is dead and tries to call him. But just before she does, she realizes what has happened and returns to her game, recording her score on another time image, "the Life / Insurance calendar." She is struck by the implication and jests: "*Sol, . . . Sol, /* If you will help me, I will win the world." In response, she sees only a young boy blowing dandelion pollen in the air and her thoughts wander off again.

This time, together with Harry, she returns to spring and the pagan rites of regeneration and immortality suggested by the symbol of the pollen. These rites are sensual and animalistic and so are the images which follow. Her dog, worrying "through the coils of the brush," returns the Uroboros image. He is pursued by memories of a "pileated bird" who with his bill once killed sandsnakes in the flotsam and of children, especially Anne, caught in the circling whirlpool and rockpools of the river.

It is through Adam's sin, however, that they entered the lifetime cycle, and it is through Jehovah, not Zeus, that they must achieve salvation. She understood this and should have conveyed it to Harry in their marriage. In failing to do so, she has killed a part of herself. To regain this part as priestess of salvation, her mind returns her to a world turned Avernus, where, seeing herself as a new Persephone, she tells of her escape from the Hades of her childhood. Adopted by the Kavanaughs, she grows up on their estate and eventually falls in love with Harry. On their wedding night, aware of their responsibility to the past, they vow to restore the woods of Kavanaugh to their children. This vow proves meaningless, and her mind telescopes through the guilt-ridden, childless years of their marriage to Harry's retirement from the Navy. Having failed to accomplish either the restoration of the woods or the generation of their line, they spend this retirement, the whole of World War II, at home, viewing the empty countryside at harvest. Thus, she has failed in her simplest function as priestess of salvation, as the means of bodily regeneration suggested by the boys and the dandelion pollen. As a result, Harry is dispirited and she tries vainly to revive him.

Christmas, for Christians the time of the birth of the Redeemer, portrays Harry caught up by the same forces—family tradition—which damned "Adam" in "Between the Porch and the Altar." The snow outside is being cleaned by a snowplow which as "a clowning dragon" again evokes the serpent-Uroboros image. That night, Anne dreams that she is having an affair with another man. Through her garbled dream utterances, Harry realizes the situation and tries to kill her, thinking the man is real. He recovers in time, only to have his mind permanently affected. She faints and dreams a second time. Afterward, his body and mind, depressed by failures, degenerate, while she pampers him ineffectually through the spring and summer.

Autumn again, and the new Persephone returns to Hades. She dreams that her luck at cards—like Orpheus' lute—has brought back her husband from the dead, thus breaking his life-time cycle and bringing him into immortality. In her mind she celebrates this, then awakens and tries anew to summarize the Kavanaugh achievements, seeing in the distance the room where Harry's mother worked to save the mills. She explains that even in religion she has failed: "He died outside the church / Like Harry Tudor." She is ashamed that they spent so much of their lives attempting to escape death and wonders, at their failures, why: "Why must we mistrust / Ourselves with Death who takes the world on trust?" Her answer lies in a complete acceptance of death: "And for no other reason, Love, I gave / Whatever brought me gladness to the grave." Thus like Daphne who escaped Apollo, she eludes "Sol," her Bible.

Because of Lowell's inability to find a structure that will handle its parts, the poem is the weakest in the volume. The logic is confused, and the plot suffers from a noticeable repetition and lack of buildup. Some of the recollections are not pertinent and could be cut. Others remain vague and perplexing, and the transitional devices are repetitious and mechanical. As the whole, justified perhaps by the theme of the poem, is a presentation of the compulsive repetitiousness of man, it offers little besides its gothic machinery to entice a reader.

Despite these inadequacies, the poem's acceptance of Death resolves once and for all on a worldly level the alternative of escape from the life-time cycle posed in "Between the Porch and the

Altar." The fact that Lowell offers a worldly substitute in this volume is significant. It indicates, at least, that he is no longer compelling all mankind to accept his view of contemplation as the necessary and only means of regaining God's likeness. Sympathetically, he seems to be reaching out to those whose lives may be best described as active and whose minds cannot comprehend the necessary abstraction of contemplation, people whose lives are contingent on events, and who, were they left without them, would have no lives. His reaching out to these people eliminates much from the wrenchings which filled his first volumes.

As the poem seeks no contemplative Truth or ecstasy, it completes the cycle of the religious direction in Lowell's work, the several sources of which include the contemplative tradition of St. Bernard and St. Bonaventure. The poet has abandoned one of these sources—religious .contemplation—for the successful continuation of the others. This change, which some historians of drama designate "the exclusion of the deity from drama," is often termed by them the beginning of the real tragic vision, the point at which ritual becomes motivated human action.

CHAPTER SEVEN

End of a Venture

Life Studies (1959) continues Lowell's noncontemplative pursuit of plot and character and marks further changes in the religious concepts and structure behind his poetic style. These changes, mainly reflecting the view of sensuous man reached in the closing lines of "The Mills of the Kavanaughs," lead to the obliteration in the volume of what Allen Tate called "the memory of the spiritual dignity of man, now sacrificed to mere secularization and a craving for mechanical order." This obliteration forces Lowell to evaluate and modify his techniques under his old structure so as to come closer to what he wants to say and then to abandon the structure altogether. The results are most noticeable in Sections I and III, in which a new, recurrent animal imagery signals the loss of spiritual dignity and indicates a worldly, animal existence of man, while the structure of the poems still preserves some of Lowell's earlier characteristic forms. Man is constantly compared to creatures of habit, suggesting the loss of free will and the determinism of the obliterated spiritual purpose inherent in Anne Kavanaugh's final acceptance of death. In addition, with this acceptance of death and man's subsequent loss of spirituality, the automatic exclusion of contemplation as a means of regaining God's likeness leads to the elimination of minutely realized detail indicative of meditational poetry. These details, which once contributed to Lowell's inverted baroque style, were important only as they led to an escape theology and, as in the case of "The Mills of the Kavanaughs," could prove cumbersome to the other facets of a poem's meaning. Their elimination results in an overall simplifying and tightening of techniques in Lowell's new character portrayals, but not to any lessening of his pessimistic world view.

The immediate effect of both these changes in religious concepts and structure can be seen by comparing the first stanza of "The Banker's Daughter" as it appeared in *The Partisan Review* (1954), when Lowell had changed his view of man but not his contemplative structure, and its revised version in *Life Studies*, when both have been changed. The two versions portray Marie de Medici in "cow" images, suggesting her worldly, animal nature; but the revised version retains only the last five of the original twenty-six lines. The difference—echoing the earlier meditational form—is that the earlier version, as part of its structure, places the reader where the event occurred. This requires a listing of all the conditions at work, both "Guise and Huguenot." Yet by implication neither version is intended to be contemplative, and the inclusion of such abundant detail confuses the structure. In addition, the intensely personal conclusion of both versions is negated by the formal, public opening of the original. By reducing the amount of detail to what is pertinent to the poem's plot—the conditions of the royal family—the second version with its single, colloquial tone terminates in a clearer, more flexible, more immediate, and unified historical portrait which, if adapted to other poems and themes, would permit a wider range of plot and character than was possible in *The Mills of the Kavanaughs*.

Simultaneous with these changes and perhaps as a justification of them is the appearance of a new, worldly aesthetic deriving much of its framework from the aesthetic ideas of Ezra Pound, particularly his definitions of style and culture in *Guide to Kulchur* (1938), but still preserving Lowell's own desires for an ideal, all-inclusive poetry. Style, for Lowell, becomes now a matter of "so knowing words that one will communicate the various parts of what one says with the various degrees and weights of importance which one wishes," and culture "is what you can pick up and/or get in touch with, by talk with the most intelligent men of the period." "The history of a culture is the history of ideas going into action." Furthermore, as Lowell indicates in his review of John Berryman's 77 *Dream Songs* (1964)—if not in his review of Robert Penn Warren's *Brother to Dragons* (1953), where he mentions usury and statistics—Pound's aesthetic ideas are a continuation of his interest in "repoeticizing": "From Pound he [Berryman] learned the all-inclusive style, the high spirits, the flitting from subject to subject, irreverence and humor." As Harold H. Watts mentions in his *Ezra Pound and the Cantos* (London, 1953), behind the Poundian inclusiveness lies the same Martha-Mary distinction of contemplation which Lowell cites: "Mary sits at the feet of the Lord, the supreme and unique instant, and practices adoration; and Martha works to get the meal on the table. Pound, in mid-career, came to the conclusion that his lot (as a poet) was the task of getting the meal on the table: something that had not been done properly for generations."

Still it would be deceptive to conclude that the colloquial tone and the idea of culture, the imagery and the loose metrical structure of the poems in *Life Studies* are simply derivative. In the *Cantos* Pound transforms culture into talking; in these poems Lowell does not. Stephen Spender's comments in "Robert Lowell's Family Album" (1959) are particularly right: "Where even in Pound an anecdote remains poetically unresolved in the surface of the cantos, Lowell is able to make from the anecdote a language like mosaic." The "mosaic" is explained by Hugh B. Staples: "One reason for the somewhat immobile quality of many of these poems is to be found in Lowell's great dependence on inanimate physical detail. One line from 'Beyond the Alps': 'Life changed to landscape,' could in this sense serve as an epigraph for the volume as a whole. Individual titles ... suggest the increasing importance of places in Lowell's life and work." He goes on to define the motive behind this use of physical detail as a reflection of Lowell's quest for permanence and as a means of illuminating character, but it would seem that some of this attention to physical detail, like the structure of certain poems, may be merely a carryover from his meditational practices.

Moreover, behind the poems of *Life Studies* and the techniques of both Lowell and Pound lie epic visions which incorporate three common important principles: communication, history, and love. These principles explain other changes in Lowell's work. As Roy Harvey Pearce points out in *The Continuity of American Poetry* (Princeton, 1961), at bottom Pound's belief (and Lowell's new practice) "would make possible his kind of epic: one in which degrees and weights would be so finely managed that communication ... would be exact and exacting knowledge. The end ... the new Paideuma ["ideas in action"] . . . would, again, make the new man." Like Whitman's epic hero, this man must be created, not confirmed, and, although like Lowell, Pound believes a concept of God "is somewhere in sight in all poetry," behind his creation is not St. Augustine's City of God, but a study of history. According to Pound, "The capitalist imperialist state must be judged not only in comparison with unrealized utopias, but with past forms of the state; if it will not bear comparison with the feudal order; with the small city states both republican and despotic; either as to its 'social justice' *or* as to its permanent products, art, science, literature, the onus of proof goes against it." In Lowell this shift from his earlier hopes for "a society with a Catholic framework" is indicated in "Beyond the Alps" when he writes: "I left the City of God where it belongs." In "Ford Madox Ford" it prompts his "selling short" the kind of esoteric taste which resulted in Ford's dying "in want." As with Pound's midcareer decision, communication not communion is his aim. Finally, as Pearce comments on Pound: "If history is ideas in action, the act is one of love—by which the poet and his protagonists, out of some sublime necessity, have been created." For Lowell this is a shift from contemplative love to human love, which most religious commentators regard as the first step toward and from higher kinds of love. It is as if Lowell has discovered that he has begun too high on the scale of love and must take a step backward to insure at least this basic response.

"Beyond the Alps," the first poem of the volume, composed in the new, slack style without recourse to myth to lend it overall importance, texture, and form, shows the effects of these changes in its insistence on worldly occurrence and its emphasis on history as "ideas in action." The title derives from the half-line in "Falling Asleep over the Aeneid," in which Lowell suggests the forces at work against Rome. Now on a train between Rome and Paris, he pictures these forces—mainly ideological—against a landscape which is both actual and symbolic. The movement of the train up and down the Alps, hurrying to complete its journey, reflects Western civilization—Etruria, Rome, Paris—hurrying to complete its identity in the same up-down motion. As defined by Lowell, the forces are human understanding, which yearly reduces occurrences from the realm of the miraculous to the realm of the scientific. Modern man, no longer able to cope with mystery or the past, is reluctantly carried along in this motion of civilizations. The motion—the rise and fall of civilizations indicated in the various mountain peaks—typifies the pattern of all history and repeats the cyclical view of history suggested earlier in "Napoleon Crosses the Beresina." It also introduces the first of the volume's many determined, "copeless" heroes.

Set after an unsuccessful attempt to climb Mt. Everest in the year that Pope Pius XII saw no conflict between dogma and science and proclaimed the dogma of the bodily assumption of Mary, the poem outlines these tensions. Everest, the last mountain to challenge man's sense of wonder with its height, symbolizes the Olympus of ancient Greece. With its conquest, the mind would have conquered the sense of wonder and reduced all to "Minerva, the miscarriage of the brain." Against this possibility, the Pope is pictured setting the people astir with his announcement. Yet behind his office is the man whose electric razor and pet canary are signs of his having fallen victim also to the conveniences of modern scientific technology.

The structure of the poem follows the narrative sweep of the train ride and is epical only in fragments. At one point, Mussolini is compared with Caesar, and the poet is compared throughout with Roman patriots. But even at the poem's close, where most of the allusions occur, no clearly drawn epic parallel emerges: Apollo, like Odysseus, burns out the Alp's eye; Minerva, who has guided other epic figures (Telamachus, Jason, Diomedes), now guides the traveler; and Paris, portrayed as a kind of Borgia king, poisons Rome and what she stands for, replacing her as the center of culture. None establishes a direct parallel of past and present. All signify, however, a significant ideological change from the poet's earlier view in "Dea Roma" that Catholic mysticism and the City of God were the static measures of man's social framework. Here Pound's "past forms of the state" seems to have been introduced. In addition, the lack of Uroboros, serpent, Satan, and Adam seem to suggest that the religious maelstrom which earlier had led Lowell to force most of his poems into the same contemplative structure may have disappeared.

An earlier magazine version of the poem, longer and more detailed, contained long sections devoted to the death of American philosopher-poet George Santayana in Rome, explanations of his apostasy, and a picture of a politically wrought-up Italy reflecting Santayana's comments on Fascism in *Dominations and Powers*

(1951). The dying Santayana, like the departing traveler, represents the dying sense of wonder in the world and another sort of departure from Rome. Other sections of the earlier version portrayed the death of Western civilization through still another aspect of Roman history—militarism—and indicated a revival of Lowell's intense interest in politics, which was largely missing from *The Mills of the Kavanaughs*. Though accurate and helpful in letting the reader imagine all aspects of the event, these sections reflected not so much the dichotomy of religion and science but side issues which confused the major issues of the poem. Their omission makes for a more unified work, although occasional comments of the poem still remain disparate. Some of the omitted sections have been revised as a separate poem, "For George Santayana." Others have subsequently been reinstated.

Lowell brings his discussion of love into historical perspective in "the banker's daughter," Marie de Medici, who crossed the Alps three centuries earlier to make her home in Paris as the second wife of Henri IV. As envisioned by Lowell, she differs from the opposing portraits drawn by a writer for *The Catholic Encyclopedia* and by some French historians. The first sees her as a protectoress of Catholicism: "The policy of Henri IV, who, had he lived, would have striven more and more to secure alliances with Protestant powers, was replaced by a Catholic policy, aiming at a Spanish alliance." Jacques Boulenger, in *The Seventeenth Century*, sees her as "obese, sensual, the low forehead shaded by the frizzled fair hair, the prominent short-sighted eyes, the red and white complexion of a fat overfed woman," whose "chief thought, when she heard of his [Henri's] death, was that now she would be able to spend as freely as she chose." Like Anne Kavanaugh, Lowell's Queen has accepted Death, and her "tragic" vision, if one can call it that, is of her own sensual nature and her inability to see beyond the pleasures of physical love. With this vision and her own inability to cope with her natural drives comes an understanding of her adulterous husband: "If ever you took / unfair advantages by right of birth, / pardon the easy virtues of the earth."

The poem catches the Queen as she is trying to come to grips with herself and rule France after her husband's assassination by François Ravaillac. She feels the king's policy of religious toleration has significantly weakened the power of the throne and led to his death at the supposed hire of the Jesuits. But her own worldliness and her dependence upon her lover, Concino Concini, assassinated in turn in 1617 by suggestion of Louis XIII, represents a poor substitute. Echoing several poems, notably "The Mills of the Kavanaughs," the poem outlines her recollections of their marriage. Extravagant, sensual, she has driven her husband from their marriage bed with her wranglings, and he who feared death in war dies instead at the hand of an assassin. "Murder cut him short— / a kitchen-knife honed on a carriage-wheel." Finally, she has taken up with the ambitious Concini, whom she resorts to in the closing lines of the poem before she asks forgiveness of her husband. Thus, when strength or decision is needed, she, too, is ultimately "helpless," and her acceptance of death is her consolation for this failing.

Set some time after the assassination, so that the Queen is no longer concerned about her own safety, the poem relies mainly on the character of the Queen and the strength of the situation to carry its tensions. The result is not a complete success. Her indecision as to whether her primary concern is "king must follow king" or love, and the subsequent conflict between formal and informal situations result in a rather unresolved narrative which is helped neither by technique nor dramatic sense. In technique, Lowell seems to apply Thomas Jefferson's dictum on best government to his poetry—"that skill is best which governs least," and the result is a breezy, sympathetic, unmajestic diction which shows little contrivance on the poet's part. The lines build sparsely and completely into a series of tableaux which drift to their end without the marshaling overall image patterns and word interplay of his earlier poems.

The attention to dramatic sense is even slacker. There is no clearly defined incident for the monologue, and this results in a further sense of arbitrariness in the urgency out of which the dramatic conflict evolves. The arbitrariness produces additional adverse effects. Marie de Medici does not have enough atmosphere, physical or cultural, to assume a life independent of the poet, or, like the hero of "Beyond the Alps," to be a real transient in this drifting series of tableaux. Neither Henri nor Sully appear to bolster her character by offering a contrast to her own indecision. Consequently, for one used to the rich techniques of Lowell's meditational style and to the immediacy of Lowell's successfully motivated character poems, this poem seems flat. The reader is never quite certain where he has been or why it is important for him to have been there.

Nevertheless, the poem's real contribution is its emphasis on worldly love, on the basis of which Marie de Medici appeals to her husband for forgiveness and understanding. This appeal suggests a solution to injustice which is different from the solutions of "At the Indian Killer's Grave" and "David and Bathsheba in the Public Garden." There, at the Last Judgment, the transgressed judged their transgressors. In this new solution with its worldly emphasis, hope as well as understanding spring in the human breast.

In its examination of contemporary America, "Inauguration Day: January 1953" turns to historical interests and the cyclical view of man in "Beyond the Alps." The poem is again based on a comparison between the present and "past forms of the state," not the City of God, and in this sense reflects the new aesthetic. Yet it has elements of the old. Portraying a culture which in times of peace has called military men to rule, the poem outlines the consequences of these callings as they fill the streets of New York City. All the calls have failed. Stuyvesant, made timeless in his statue, betrayed his trust when he surrendered New Amsterdam in 1664. His administration was not successful. Likewise Grant, represented by his famous tomb, had not served successfully enough to rescue his name from the political scandals which rocked his second term in office. Now Eisenhower has been called to rule and to take his place someday among the landmarks of the city. The analogy, apparent from the start, is that Ike, too, will fail as an administrator. The place for embalming is prepared, and it resembles Dante's last circle of Hell. Epical rather than dramatic in its vision, the picture suggests the style, theme, tone, structure, and language of Lowell's wartime prophecies and indicates anew the harshness with which he can write if he so chooses.

"A Mad Negro Soldier Confined at Munich," the last poem of the first section, details another study of love in the ramblings of its demented hero—love here being opposed by situation. In this respect the poem seems to echo the same life-time cycles of Lowell's earlier poetry, except that it rightly conceives of the escape, not as one of salvation but as one of physical love: "Who but my girl-friend set the town on fire?" For the hero, God does not exist, nor do the realms of mysticism which occupied the earlier studies. The

Negro is seeking personal and "human" intercourse with the Fräulein who stitches "outing shirts" in the colored wards. In her lies his escape: "I had her six times in the English Garden." As a result, he resembles not epic heroes but animals and machines: he is a fancy minnow in the air-conditioned bowl, a slave to habit who cannot see beyond the world of sensation; or, like the switch to some machine, his girl-friend provides the spark of his existence: "Oh mama, mama, like a trolley-pole / sparking at contact, her electric shock— / the power-house!" On this level of awareness, he conceives of his confinement as a boxing match in which he has just been floored and senses the futility of the fight which will spring him from it: "Rounds, rounds! Why punch the clock?" Fire, traditionally associated with mystical as well as physical love, represents in the poem the opposing power that unites. Forced upon him by his nature, faults, and ambitions, the conflict of the two—his need for love and his surroundings—he sees, like Marie de Medici, as a conflict against which he is substantially helpless.

He emerges from the conflict as a forceful and fully drawn character, and the poem is one of the most successful of Lowell's nightmarish monologues. Part of the reason is that the immediate cause of the conflict is given as "the boys who floored me," and the outburst seems justified. Likewise, in that the poem realizes its surroundings more vividly than does "The Banker's Daughter," its actions resemble the meditational exercises of *The Mills of the Kavanaughs*, and Lowell appears more at ease with them. This is reflected especially in his wit in taking love images and metaphors which have been appropriated by mystical poetry and returning them to physical love with all their acquired mystical connotations. Intimate, colloquial, the poem is kept alive by tensions of situation and technique and by the various "degrees and weights" of exact words rather than by any superimposed rhetorical pattern. In addition, by the hero's giving in to habit, it suggests the fullness of an action which is complete and repetitious by nature—more fights, more love, more rounds—and which the poet, having suggested, wishes to leave only as a suggestion.

Although such poems may succeed individually, their failure as a group to assert a new clear aesthetic, or to reject the old one when they do not succeed, has caused reviewers to dismiss the entire section as "transitional." Thom Gunn, in *The Yale Review* (1960), even goes so far as to say: "They read, in fact, like parodies. The familiar bumps and grinds communicate no passion, and the poems are like the works of a slavish and unimaginative disciple." Still, they do break with the restricted forms of Lowell's previous volume and look forward, as Gunn remarks, to the "interesting departures in subject-matter" and the "surprising style" of the later sections.

After a prose, autobiographical segment, "91 Revere Street," the volume resumes its poetic study of character in Section III with character sketches of four writers—Ford Madox Ford, George Santayana, Delmore Schwartz, and Hart Crane—all of whom are like the mad Negro soldier in being caught up in a variation of the old life-time cycle. In them no new concept of man emerges; all are as compulsive about their writing and as "carried-along" by instinct as the characters of the opening section. Yet behind their constrictions lie two new principles: the immortality of art as "ideas in action," and communication as the basis of this immortality and metamorphosis. Lowell's earlier view of the poet as illuminator of the Divine, like his earlier view of the City of God as the illumination, has been replaced by life illuminations and not only "unrealized utopias" but "past forms of the state."

Concerned with this pursuit of immortality, the poems offer telling contrasts to Lowell's earlier views of salvation. Formerly, he tried to merge art and religion into one experience by fusing the techniques of meditation with those of artistic creation and by letting the principles of his religious vision overpower his artistic technique. Now, having divorced the processes of art and religion and having assumed a more worldly aesthetic, he investigates art's pursuit of immortality alone and opposes this pursuit to society's attempt to stifle the artist. Thus, the poems coming to grips with art offer a fine contrast to "In Memory of Arthur Winslow" coming to grips with life on religious terms. The descriptions are illuminative rather than evocative, and each separate sketch contains several incidents rather than the single, focused events of that poem. The observer who is "illuminated" rather than what is observed furnishes the continuity of the whole. Indicative of the new worldly interest in art, Hart Crane, not the Virgin Mary, delivers the final, "truthful" colloquy. Gone are the once tightly worked epical structures; only the poem "For George Santayana" connects in any way with religion.

The first poem of the section, "Ford Madox Ford," depicts

the youthful idealism of the would-be writer who sees art only as something "that made the great your equals" and who is not yet fully committed to its truth. This truth is symbolized in Ford. Because of his "breadth of view, immense knowledge of many literatures, and an unwavering loyalty to his great profession," Caroline Gordon, in "The Story of Ford Madox Ford," designates him as "perhaps the last great man of letters in the nineteenth century style." Based on personal reminiscence and fragments from one of Ford's memoirs, *It Was the Nightingale* (1933), the poem is the most successful of the group in achieving the purposes of plot, character, and illumination. Longer, more incisive, and more distinctive in diction than the others, it portrays the English novelist (whose original family name was Hueffer) on the golf-links with Lloyd George. In this portrait, with its fish images, Ford greatly resembles Miss Gordon's description of him: "For several minutes there was no sound in the room except his labored breathing. I remember thinking that he looked like a big white whale as he sat there, forcing the breaths through his wide-open mouth. Suddenly he looked up. The fishlike gaze brightened." In Lowell's poem, however, the phrase "filthy art," not the fish images, forms the clue to the poem.

> *The lobbed ball plops, then dribbles to the cup....*
> *(a birdie Fordie!) But it nearly killed*
> *the ministers. Lloyd George was holding up*
> *the flag. He gabbled, "Hop-toad, hop-toad, hop-toad!*
> *Hueffer has used a niblick on the green;*
> *it's filthy art, Sir, filthy art!"*

Concerned with the circumstances which produced *The Good Soldier*, "the best French novel in the language," the poem recalls the world's attempts to stifle Ford. Five times he was "blackballed for promotion" before he was "mustard gassed voiceless some seven miles / behind the lines at Nancy." But he defied death and the "whale-fat of post-war London," by going first to France and then to New York and writing his way into life. This writing which made him the equal of Lloyd George left him unpopular and relatively unread: "But master, mammoth mumbler, tell me why / the bales of your left-over novels buy / less than a bandage for your gouty foot." Despite this unpopularity, Ford, in a pun on Hueffer, puffs on, described, as were the characters of the first section, in animal imagery and addressed by Lowell in a final colloquy reminiscent of the addresses he made earlier to Arthur Winslow in his contemplative poems.

The address makes clear that Lowell's view of artistic communication as his medium of mysticism forces him to reject Ford's limited popularity as a proper escape from time into immortality:

> *Wheel-horse, O unforgetting elephant,*
> *I hear you huffing at your old Brevoort,*
> *Timon and Falstaff, while you heap the board*
> *for publishers. Fiction! I'm selling short*
> *your lies that made the great your equals. Ford,*
> *you were a kind man and you died in want.*

But by this rejection Lowell provides the illumination of a writer's proper means to immortality and his necessary perseverance. Consequently, the brief glimpse of the golf episode is not only remarkably effective as a characterization of Ford, but it is personally beneficial to the observer. The extent of its beneficence, however, is not fully determined until "Words for Hart Crane."

Wonderfully sympathetic and ironic, "For George Santayana" takes as its subject the implied idealism and dedication of "Ford Madox Ford" and seems to answer the question of how far a writer should go in pursuit of truth. Santayana, who regarded himself as both "an atheist and a Catholic," rejected, in pursuit of his own orthodoxy, the theology of Catholicism. His discussion of this apostasy in *Reason in Religion* proves particularly relevant: "Even the heretics and atheists, if they have had profundity, turn out after a while to be forerunners of some new orthodoxy. What they rebel against is a religion alien to their nature; they are atheists only by accident, and relatively to a convention which inwardly offends them, but they yearn mightily in their own souls after the religious acceptance of a world interpreted in their own fashion." Thus, by extension, the writer in conflict with his religious beliefs in pursuit of truth seems justified in thinking of himself as a forerunner of a new orthodoxy.

Using nothing but taut vision to unify its incidents, the poem proceeds to fill with knowing strokes a picture of Rome in 1952, with Santayana on his deathbed in the foreground, working diligently to revise the galley proofs of his last book. As indicated, some of the poem's sections appeared as parts of the first version of

"Beyond the Alps." Now, making clear Lowell's rejection of the dramatic form of Joyce and Nietzsche in which characters "assume a proper and intangible esthetic life," the poem seeks a different end in its second-person presentation. Comprised of personal reminiscence as well as snatches of published letters, it uses Santayana as a "sounding board" for the observer and stresses only the drama of the situation at hand and its resulting illumination.

Lowell offers no happy escapes in the poem. Santayana is portrayed as close to the Church and as having chosen the walls of her monasteries to die in, wishing the "geese-girl sisters wouldn't bother / their heads and yours by praying for your soul." In that closeness he has insisted "the Church was too good to be believed" and sought his immortality through his writings. As a result, his pursuit of truth has made him at once an unbeliever and a martyr. And thus the poem presents its metaphors of pursuit—Daphne by Apollo, the Pythian Feast, the green cloth by Ser Brunetto—and recognizes in the image of Ser Brunetto, who smiles as if he has won, the probable damnation of Santayana. All the same, there are no recriminations and none of the vindictiveness of presentation which marred character studies in both *Lord Weary's Castle* and *The Mills of the Kavanaughs*.

The poem's "mysticism"—for Santayana a merging with his works—is pictured in the traditional bride and gold symbols of religious mysticism and suggests a view, similar to Joyce's, of the artist as consecrator of the Host. Yet, like the love imagery of "A Mad Negro Soldier Confined at Munich," the symbols signal worldly gain, the immortality of history. This is emphasized in the poem's classical allusions, which suggest Santayana's continuity with the past rather than with soulless modernity. Even "the broken-hearted lions," the poem's final animal image, are placed in the "worn arena" of the classical world. Thus, in his handling of situation and language Lowell seems to have caught successfully the ironies of the man who in an earlier version of the poem asked, "The spirit giveth life; will letters kill . . . ?" and who in both versions insists, "There is no God and Mary is his mother." Again, at the poem's end, Lowell addresses his subject, seeing him as a soldier of truth opposing perhaps the "souvenir-deranged G.I.'s and officer-professors of philosophy" who come crashing into Santayana's cell at the beginning of the poem.

"To Delmore Schwartz," the third poem of the section, takes

up the idea of the personal sacrifices, including the damnation of Santayana, and measures their effects on less wilful writers. For its subject, the man who can do nothing right, Lowell uses the composite examples of Schwartz and himself, who fail in the basics of self-preservation, and goes on to consider the fates of writers and household and social failures during a 1946 visit to Harvard: "We couldn't even keep the furnace lit!" Another of the many pictures of "copeless" heroes, the poem thus becomes the volume's first real study in perversity. As such, it relies heavily on reminiscences, which, in one instance remarkably antedate Josef Stalin's cerebral hemorrhages.

In the poem, modern technology, represented by a disconnected refrigerator, tries to destroy them; and the house, which is "mustard" yellow, reflects convention's attempt at destruction. The object of both writers is to thwart this annihilation as they sit inside talking, watched over by "angels of escape"— a duck which Schwartz killed and which looks through them "as if it'd died dead drunk," and a portrait of Samuel Taylor Coleridge displaying "a paranoid inert gaze." Mentioning Joyce, Schopenhauer, and Freud, they try after dinner to recapture for themselves the world of dreams, realizing the exacting price it sometimes requires of the poet. Citing this price, Schwartz misquotes William Wordsworth's "Resolution and Independence"—"We poets in our youth begin in sadness; / thereof in the end come despondency and madness"— and adds, "Stalin has had two cerebral hemorrhages." Outside, the Charles River, which once represented the road to afterlife, turns silver in the moonlight as the two writers talk on and drink into the ebb-light of morning.

Reminiscent of "The Death of the Sheriff," the poem seems to say that through insanity, death, and alcohol, the writer breaks the strangleholds of his surroundings and that, aware of the dangers in these methods, Schwartz and Lowell have accepted the risk. Written after the mental breakdowns of both writers, the poem not only provides a poignant plea for understanding but also tries to rescue itself from bathos by a sense of whimsy and a sinister foreknowledge which resembles Achilles' promise of immortality in the *Iliad*. It seems to say that men live by pursuing their fates. In this statement and its resulting "heroic" illumination, Lowell nowhere assumes the prophetic and epical egoism of his early poetry. There are no classical parallels and the illumination, like his technique, remains comically low key. All in all, it is the weakest poem of the section. The emphasis it places on clarity, the accurate and unmistakable exactness of its language, and the devices of fore-knowledge and whimsy are not enough to rescue it whole heartedly from bathos or mere personal anecdote.

"Words for Hart Crane," the last of the four poems on art, has the writer answer the question of the worth of these sacrifices to artistic truth and self-preservation. Open, frank, sometimes offensive, it reveals a man who has no regrets for having sacrificed himself to poetry and returns the reader more overtly to the Dionysian concerns of *The Mills of the Kavanaughs*. Again, as in the opening section, these concerns are rightly seen as an escape not to God, but to history and cultural immortality. The escape is signaled in the last line, where "laying the heart out" utilizes as an immortalizing process Sir James Frazer's description in *The Golden Bough* of Dionysian immortality rites. These pagan rites replace Christ's coming to fetch the soul in Lowell's earlier poems and suggest the non-Christian element of the process. In addition, the nature of the colloquy, which functions like the last section of "In Memory of Arthur Winslow," reveals the poet's success in achieving "ideas in action." Thus, the poet breaks the cycle of his existence not by religious meditation but by giving himself completely to his craft. By such means he escapes the poem's Apollonian world of "Pulitzers," tradition, and "gold-plated laurels."

Originally intended for some unspecified English poet, the poem is now spoken by Hart Crane as an explanation of his actions and of the methods by which he became *Catullus redivivus*, from his love of Whitman's poetry to his own homosexuality. None of Crane's pretensions to mysticism enter the poem—only his attempts to communicate on a worldly plane, either through poetry or love. This emphasizes the view expressed earlier in "Ford Madox Ford" that rapport with one's fellowman and not with God is the basis of man's new escape from time. Despite this, the poem is more committed to earlier forms, voices, themes, and techniques than are the others in the section. The sonnet form seems to defeat the expressed long-poem intention of the character poem. The voice resembles Lowell's more than Crane's, and rather than "drawn," the message is "delivered." Likewise, in its listing of methods and its harsh views of American society, the poem gives merely notional assent to character analysis and offers instead a steamshiplike travelogue to artistic immortality. Still, as with many Lowell poems, its strength is the distinctive energy of Lowell's peculiar approach.

In short then, these poems which outline Lowell's coming to grips with art show that his new ideas have only begun to encroach upon his old thought patterns. The new emphasis on exact words, the loss of minutely realized detail, the principles of history, communication, and love have added up to a new emphasis on the active and worldly rather than the contemplative man. This new view of man reflected in the animal imagery which Lowell attaches to Ford Madox Ford, Delmore Schwartz, Hart Crane, and possibly George Santayana, still purposes escape from time, but now not into salvation but into cultural history. Moreover, Lowell still seems to think of poetry in terms of events rather than as freely juxtaposed poetic images.

Nonetheless, the ideas have entailed certain changes. Lowell has abandoned his plot and character poems for poems of illumination, and except for a lingering epical structure, he has almost completely broken with his earlier ideas of art. These changes Lowell summarizes in a *Paris Review* interview (1961): "My last poems don't use religious imagery, they don't use symbolism. In many ways they seem to me more religious than the early ones, which are full of symbols and references to Christ and God. . . . Yet I don't feel my experience changed very much. It seems to me it's clearer to me now than it was then, but it's very much the same sort of thing that went into the religious poems—the same sort of struggle, light and darkness, the flux of experience. The morality seems much the same."

The summary is deceptive, for although the morality is the same, religiously Lowell has changed to a position which not only portrays but understands aspects of the active life. The contemplative threads and now the archetypal framework of meditation have been eliminated. What he keeps is a fluid, adaptable style which places communication and diversity of character above all else. But behind this lurks a tendency to view such diversity as a lack of spirituality and to picture people in animal images. Lowell needs to take a new look at himself, and in the final section of the volume the effect of this look is a long smoldering break with Joycean ideas.

∧

CHAPTER EIGHT

Life Studies

As a group the poems which comprise the last section of *Life Studies,* giving the book its title, are the real achievement of the volume. They put an end to the "mythic" vision Lowell derives from writers like James Joyce and to the hold this vision has had on his poetry. No longer, as T. S. Eliot suggested, will Lowell be confined to the one "method of controlling, of ordering, of giving shape and a significance to the immense panorama of futility and anarchy which is contemporary history," behind which would lie his single view of the poet as divine illuminator. As Stephen Spender remarks: "He [Lowell] has taken a lot of facts, observed or remembered (each of them strikingly separate as brittle shape or anecdote) and made from them his own truth. . . . What these poems point to is the possibility of a humanist kind of poetry, in which disparate experiences are bound up within a poet who has himself an immense compassion combined with clearness and hardness."

Lowell's difficulty in reaching the point where he can discard this technique recalls T. S. Eliot's remarks in his 1936 essay, "A Note on the Verse of John Milton." Here Eliot suggests that Milton was too towering a genius over his contemporaries and had too great an effect on young writers and ends the essay by comparing Milton's genius to Joyce's. The comparison permits by extension an assumption of the dangers to young writers of Joyce and his mythic literature. These dangers are rather clearly defined in Mary McCarthy's devastating analysis of recent American fiction in "Settling the Colonel's Hash" (1954):

What is depressing about this insistent symbolization is the fact that while it claims to lead to the infinite, it quickly reaches very finite limits—there are only so many myths on record, and once you have got through Bulfinch, the Scandinavian, and the Indian, there is not much left.... American fiction of the symbolist school demonstrates this mournful truth, without precisely intending to. A few years ago... chic novels and stories fell into three classes: those which had a Greek myth for their framework, which the reader was supposed to detect, like finding the faces in the clouds in old newspaper puzzle contests; those which had symbolic modern figures, dwarfs, hermaphrodites, and cripples, illustrating maiming and loneliness; and those which contained symbolic animals, cougars, wild cats, and monkeys.

The dangers are partly responsible for the maelstrom of Lowell's imagination in his second and third volumes of poetry and his inability finally to deal with a whole range of twentieth-century experience, either because he could find no epic parallels or because, when he did, the parallels distorted his impression.

With this break and with the continuation of the Poundian aesthetics begun in the earlier sections of the book is an abandoning of poems constructed along a linear sequence of events and consequently of poems of plot. What is employed instead is the "time-shift" device of Ford Madox Ford. As Hugh Kenner states in *The Poetry of Ezra Pound* (London, 1951): "The function of the time-shift is to do away with the plot—plot in the sense of a linear sequence of events. The 'story' is broken up into a number of scenes, conversations, impressions, etc., which function as poetic images and are freely juxtaposed for maximum intensity." It is a technique which Ford uses quite effectively in his memoirs, especially in *It Was the Nightingale*, from which Lowell obtained some of the information for his "Ford Madox Ford." To illustrate the technique and its similarity to Lowell's new vision requires long quotations from both writers, but principally the similarities reside in cadence, metaphor, ellipses (their own in both cases), and in the kind of associations on which their time shifts are based. The first quotation is from *It Was the Nightingale:*

I stood then alone and feeling conspicuous—a heavy blond man in a faded uniform in those halls of France. Pale faces swam, inspectantly, toward me. But, as you may see fishes do round a bait in dim water, each one checked suddenly and swam away with a face expressing piscine distaste. I imagined that the barb of a hook must protrude somewhere from my person and set myself to study the names and romantic years of the wines that M. Berthelot had provided for us.

Their juice had been born on vines, beneath suns of years before these troubles and their names made fifty sweet symphonies. . . . It had been long, long indeed, since I had so much as thought of even such minor glories as *Château Neuf du Pape* or *Tavel* or *Hermitage*—though I think White Hermitage of a really good vintage year the best of all white wines. . . . I had almost forgotten that there were any potable liquids but *vins du pays* and a horrible fluid that we called Hooch. The nine of diamonds used to be called the curse of Scotland, but surely *usquebaugh*—which tastes like the sound of its name—is Scotland's curse to the world . . . . and to Scotland. That is why Glasgow on a Saturday night is Hell. . . .

A long black figure detached itself from Mr. Bennett's side and approached me. It had the aspect of an undertaker coming to measure a corpse. . . . The eyes behind enormous lenses were like black pennies and appeared to weep dimly; the dank hair was plastered in flattened curls all over the head. . . . I decided that I did not know the gentleman. His spectacles swam almost against my face. His hollow tones were those of a funeral mute:

"You used to write," it intoned, "didn't you?"

He continued—and it was as if his voice came from the vaults of Elsinore. . . .

The second is from Section IV of "My Last Afternoon with Uncle Devereux Winslow":

I picked with a clean finger nail at the blue anchor
on my sailor blouse washed white as a spinnaker.
What in the world was I wishing?
... A sail-colored horse browsing in the bullrushes ...
A fluff of the west wind puffing
my blouse, kiting me over our seven chimneys,
troubling the waters. ...
As small as sapphires were the ponds: Quittacus, Snippituit,
and Assawompset, *halved by "the Island,"*
where my Uncle's duck blind
floated in a barrage of smoke-clouds.
Double-barrelled shotguns
stuck out like bundles of baby crow-bars.
A single sculler in a camouflaged kayak
was quacking to the decoys. ...
At the cabin between the waters,
the nearest windows were already boarded.
Uncle Devereux was closing camp for the winter.
As if posed for "the engagement photograph,"
he was wearing his severe
war-uniform of a volunteer Canadian officer. ..

The effects of the time shift coupled with a loss of all efforts to regain the Christian experience produce a section of poems concerned mainly with observations of life, not with detailing the means of achieving God's likeness, and the significance of which is measured and ordered by the placement of images not by any yardstick of past events. In this respect the poems are derivative of moods similar to those which in *Lord Weary's Castle* produced "Buttercups" and "In the Cage," and, if anything, they seem to recall the efforts of W. B. Yeats's middle period, when through personal recollection he began to establish the groundwork for the elaborate personal mythology of his later poems. In essence this may be what Lowell is establishing, for nowhere in the poems does he either prevent his eventual return to "epical" structures or negate the ultimate necessity of man's religious life. He has merely selected areas and techniques which are exclusive of these concerns.

But unlike Yeats, whose personal life takes on national importance because it and his works were so wrapped up in the development of the Irish nation and literature, Lowell's life, though typifying a kind of American life, bears no comparable sense of importance. This has led to attacks on the section by critics like Joseph Bennett, in *The Hudson Review* (1959), who finds it lacking significant content: "... the whole volume is a collection of lazily recollected and somewhat snobbish memoirs, principally of the poet's own wealthy and aristocratic family. ... it is more suited as an appendix to some snobbish society magazine, to *Town and Country* or *Harper's Bazaar*, rather than a purposeful work." The attacks, however, need not effect the significance of the poems' technique nor prevent discussion of the content.

Typical of the section's new manner is the poem "For Sale," dealing with the sale of the Lowell cottage at Beverly Farms after the death of Lowell's father in 1950. The poet pictures the grief of his mother for her husband, but nowhere mentions similar scenes of grief in epic literature nor passes any moral judgments. A few years earlier he might have used the incident to parallel Andromache's grief for Hector or Anna's grief for Dido, but now his primary concern is conveying the exact nature of the loss. His presentation is direct, immediate, and homely. His setting is worldly; his technique, slack. Understatement rather than overstatement typifies his portrayal. Gone is the "immense vigor and gusto" which Conrad Aiken found in *Land of Unlikeness*. Gone, too, is the young poet who in 1947 objected to Dylan Thomas' faulty line patterns, for he would never have permitted "Ready, afraid" to stand as a complete line. But Lowell is not concerned, as he was earlier, with the metaphysical meaning of everything or the ability of the individual line to stand on its own. As "poetic images" his lines can now be freely juxtaposed and this juxtaposition rather than their content provides the significance. In twenty years of writing he seems to have learned as well to "throw away" lines as in life he seems to have learned that some values are irrelevant to contemplation and poetic structure. There are means other than description and "epicizing" to put a reader in the place where an event occurred. These means —an appropriateness of metaphor and image—are the ones he currently uses.

Metaphors which in the past were often literary and allusive are here made up of personal experience. The mother, for example, is not portrayed as Mary Winslow was, "a Cleopatra in her housewife's dress." She is as simple and as common as the expression of her loss: "As if she had stayed on a train / one stop past her desti-nation." The reader need not be a classicist to understand this com-parison. Given the character of Charlotte Lowell portrayed in this volume, it typifies her. Likewise, the voice has been simplified: the view of the furniture as having an "on tiptoe air" and of the cot-tage as a "plaything" suggests the childish nature of the poem's persona.

These metaphors and child's voice, however, become uncer-tain and completely inappropriate in the total poem. The observa-tion of the mother's wan face "mooning" at the window suggests the unfathomable mind of a child and parallels the vision which closes "My Last Afternoon with Uncle Devereux Winslow":

> *My hands were warm, then cool, on the piles*
> *of earth and lime,*
> *a black pile and a white pile. . . .*
> *Come winter,*
> *Uncle Devereux would blend to the one color.*

However, there is a startling difference. "My Last Afternoon with Uncle Devereux Winslow" is set in 1922 when Lowell was five; "For Sale," in 1950 when he is thirty-three. With this difference, the figure of "For Sale" can only fail to understand the emotions behind the poem's final "train-stop" image. In addition, behind the child's wonder lies an inappropriate sinisterness, resulting from the poem's being organized about the same extended metaphor of "Cistercians in Germany." People, like sheep, are being led to market and slaughter. In the opening line the "sheepish plaything" descrip-tion of the house indicates its role as a sheep pen from which Com-mander Lowell is led to slaughter, a fate still awaiting his wife in the "mover-undertaker" description of time.

Devoid of religious implication, Charlotte's self-centered ani-mal sense of loss opposes the endings of "In Memory of Arthur Winslow" and "Mary Winslow," poems written for Lowell's grandfather and grandmother. In those poems the souls of his heroes went triumphantly into afterlife, Arthur accompanied by the trumpeting black swan, Mary by the ringing churchbell. Here, concern is only for that longing which Charlotte must carry with her to the grave. She must face life alone and she is not certain that she can. Having found security and direction in her marriage, she has only the indirection of her life's end, and, reminiscent of the failures in "To Delmore Schwartz," she lacks the necessary powers of communication and human understanding to make out of that indirection something meaningful.

The poems in "Life Studies" are, as a group, a new approach in structure, in voice, and in metaphor to the world Lowell portrayed in rigid metaphysical terms in his previous volumes. By the elimination of the religious direction of the moral and anagogical levels, he has accepted in his nonspiritual view the portrayal of what can best be termed the "ineffectual failure." This "failure" forms the prototype of the new hero of the book, and, concerned mainly with incidents in Lowell's growing up, the section outlines four generations of such failures in the Winslow family—from Great Aunt Sarah to Lowell's infant daughter.

The opening poem of the section, "My Last Afternoon with Uncle Devereux Winslow," introduces the whole of the Winslow family and the dreams which keep them living and useful. For Lowell's parents, appearing in the opening stanza, the dream is of the social whirl of "Fontainebleau, Mattapoisett, Puget Sound," for Lowell's grandmother, of her "rose garden," for Grandfather Winslow, once described as having the heroic "craft" that netted him a million dollars, it is the collector's world of "Falling Asleep over the Aeneid," a world of snapshots, mementoes, memories. It is he who tells the dying Uncle Devereux and his wife, about to embark on a final world-tour together, "You are behaving like children." Yet there is nothing heroic or important about him. Like his daughter in "For Sale," he grasps for personal understanding, and like many members of the Winslow family he does not get it.

Recalling the heroes of Lowell's character poems, the Winslows are caught up in the *"Tockytock, tockytock"* lockstep of pre-World War I America. Their dreams, all part of an Edwardian era which has come to an end, eventually destroy them. Great Aunt Sarah, for instance, described in unrealized Christ images, is destroyed by her dream of becoming a concert pianist, and only premature death saves the devil-may-care Devereux from the collapsing world of the stock-market crash of 1929. As a family, the Winslows are doomed, and detailing the tension between their childhood dreams and subsequent failures provides the only real interest in their lives. This interest, however, has frequently been traced before in works about post-World War I disillusion. Lowell adds no more to an understanding of its effects than does William

Faulkner in *Sartoris* or Ford Madox Ford in *Parade's End*. In addition, the Winslow tensions and efforts never really leave the immediate family confines for larger social statements. The reader feels "he has been here before," and most of his interest, as a result, is clinical.

The structure of the poem follows the time-shift technique and concentrates on the tension and on the incidental observations of Lowell playing, his hands first on a pile of earth and then on a pile of lime. There is no single illumination to be drawn from the observations. Rather, the pictorial effect, suggestive of the "life studies" title of the section, lies in a patterning of metaphors of earth, water, sky, death, and stone. It recalls the "rocklike" and "perfect" impressions of "91 Revere Street": "Major Mordecai Meyers' portrait has been mislaid past finding, but out of my memories I often come on it in the setting of our Revere Street house, a setting now fixed in the mind, where it survives all the distortions of fantasy, all the blank befogging of forgetfulness. There, the vast number of remembered *things* remains rocklike. Each is in its place, each has its function, its history, its drama. There, all is preserved by that motherly care that one either ignored or resented in his youth. The things and their owners come back urgent with life and meaning—because finished, they are endurable and perfect." The picture, in addition, is far different from any of the previous Winslow portraits. Formerly, actions had painted Winslows above the usual cut of man in heroic poses. Now their actions blend like the earth, lime, and water into deathly rocklike shapes. In these shapes the Winslows are imaged, and the remaining poems in the first part of the section complete the images thus begun.

"Dunbarton" records the funeral of Devereux in the family plot at Dunbarton, New Hampshire. Recalling the earlier "Winslows fill / The granite plot and the dwarfed trees are green," the new description runs:

Failing as when Francis Winslow could count
them on his fingers,
the clump of virgin pine still stretched patchy ostrich necks
over the disused millpond's fragrantly woodstained water,
a reddish blur,
like the ever-blackening wine-dark coat
in our portrait of Edward Winslow....

Again, Lowell's child voice predominates, and simple, personal observations set the tone. His relationship with his grandfather, touched on heroically in "In Memory of Arthur Winslow," is depicted when both grandfather and grandson come to the Winslow plot to rake leaves from the graves of their dead forebears. For Winslow, who has been disappointed by Devereux's "behaving like a child," the child represents a second chance to rescue the Winslow tradition. This chance binds the two together as "father and son" and prompts the boy's cuddling in the morning "like a paramour / in my Grandfather's bed, / while he scouted about the chattering greenwood stove."

"Grandparents" pictures the farm after the deaths of both grandparents when, if it were to be accomplished, Winslow's hope of the rescued Winslow tradition would be realized. The hope, however, is not realized, and the poet, reminiscent of the rich man in Luke 16:24 and "A Prayer for My Grandfather to Our Lady," painfully entreats: "Grandpa! Have me, hold me, cherish me! / Tears smut my fingers." Disloyal still, he measures the courage of his rebellion by doodling handlebar mustaches on a picture of the last Russian czar. Combined, the two poems represent the fall of the Winslow world of antiques and of tradition, which outlasted the broken dream worlds of Sarah and Devereux, and bring out the underlying guilt of Lowell's having failed his grandfather. This guilt in various stages seems to motivate the other, separate poems of the book.

Portraying the shattered dream world of his father and mother and their days at Mattapoisett, "Commander Lowell," "Terminal Days at Beverly Farms," "Father's Bedroom," "For Sale," and "Sailing Home from Rapallo" move the sense of failure one generation closer. It is the world of "91 Revere Street," the autobiographical fragment of Part II in *Life Studies,* in which Lowell first outlined his father's failure to achieve rank and his being eventually forced out of the Navy into a more socially respectable job. Again the voice is that of a child: "Having a naval officer / for my Father was nothing to shout / about to the summer colony at 'Matt.' " Already replaced as a father image by Arthur Winslow, the "Commander" thus becomes an image of failure and embarrassment to his son and finally to his wife and himself. In "Commander Lowell," his only accomplishments are once being "successful enough to be lost / in the mob of ruling-class Bostonians," and at nineteen, having been "the youngest ensign in his class" and " 'old man' of a gunboat on the Yangtze." Both somehow are lost in his pursuit of Mattapoisett and never adequately replaced. The subsequent disillusioned human shell is all that remains to accomplish the dreams of Lowell's mother.

"Terminal Days at Beverly Farms" details the Commander's last year, having moved "to Beverly Farms / to be a two minute walk from the station, / half an hour by train from the Boston doctors." Ill from two coronaries, he has preserved his interest in naval matters, and they keep him going after his business failures:

> *Each morning at eight-thirty,*
> *inattentive and beaming,*
> *loaded with his "calc" and "trig" books,*
> *his clipper ship statistics,*
> *and his ivory slide rule,*
> *Father stole off with the* Chevie
> *to loaf in the Maritime Museum at Salem.*
> *He called the curator*
> *"the commander of the Swiss Navy."*

Away from the sea, his death is abrupt and unprotesting; his dying words to his wife are "I feel awful." Consistent with the view of "For Sale," his death is that of one who has given up his own dreams of success to follow sheepishly the "Mattapoisetts" of his wife and family. As in that poem, the death is expressed in worldly terms. Again, the poet's inability to rise above simplified diction and imagery to a comment on life is the work's most serious defect.

"Father's Bedroom" joins "For Sale" and "Terminal Days at Beverly Farms" as companion pieces. In examining the Commander's remains—the naval blue-and-white of his room, his Chinese sandals, the clear glass of his bed lamp, his book—the poet discovers the *raison d'être* of his father's life in a copy of Lafcadio Hearn's *Glimpses of Unfamiliar Japan*, given to his father as a child by his grandmother. The father first formulated his dreams of a naval career from its exotic descriptions. But reality sometimes differs from dream, and years afterward his grandmother scribbled on the flyleaf: "This book has had hard usage / on the Yangtze River, China. / It was left under an open / porthole in a storm."

"Sailing Home from Rapallo" describes the end of the Mattapoisett dream, when the poet accompanies his mother's body home from Rapallo, Italy, in 1954. Earlier yellowhammers had lulled Vergil into dreams in "Falling Asleep over the Aeneid" and Henry Ford was a major villain in "Concord," but now Ford and birds have become so commonplace as to become mere descriptive devices. The poet's concern is pattern, and when his mind wanders, death not description brings him back to Dunbarton, "Dour and dark against the blinding snowdrifts, / its black brook and fir trunks were smooth as masts." The only "unhistoric" soul there is his father, buried under his Lowell motto, "*Occasionem cognosce*," "too businesslike and pushing" among the "twenty or thirty Winslows and Starks." His mother, who never really relinquished her Winslow heritage or her father, comes home wrapped in tinfoil like an Italian festive bread, her married name significantly misspelled.

Visiting the failures of fathers upon sons, "During Fever" pictures the poet with the inadequacies of the past, worrying his daughter through a fever: " 'Sorry,' she mumbles like her dim-bulb father, 'sorry.' " The words might express the poet's own inability to live up to what had been expected of him; instead, they recall the relationship between his mother and her father. She too had fallen victim to his overbearing dream of heirs who would restore "the men / Who . . . fought the British lion to his knees," and, as a result, destroyed both her husband and her son. In her destruction, Lowell initiates the pattern for his own failure, for his world like that portrayed in "Beyond the Alps" and "Napoleon Crosses the Berezina" is one of cyclical, ghostly paradigms.

"Waking in the Blue" details his recourse to a mental hospital when his dream world becomes disrupted by reality. There a B.U. (Boston University) sophomore, Stanley, and "Bobbie" are all fighting ghosts. For the sophomore, reading *The Meaning of Meaning*, the struggle is with the ghost of nonmeaning. For Stanley, it is with old age. For "Bobbie," who "swashbuckles about in his birthday suit," it is with aging itself. Finally, for the poet, it is his inability to live up to past dreams and his subsequent sense of guilt.

Outlining Lowell's return after a stay in the mental hospital, "Home After Three Months Away" pictures the alteration which his life has tried to effect. Having undergone treatment, he reaches out now for a direction which will veer to the future not to the past. As he explains, he "cannot loiter here / in lather like a polar bear." Cured, he is like lilies in Luke (12:27), or the forgotten headstones of his first poem, "The Park Street Cemetery," "frizzled, stale and small."

This then is the new image of the Winslow family. From it emerges the next variation of the former time-bound hero. No longer is he to be caught in the moral lockstep of time, seeking his salvation or artistic immortality. He is now caught up in the hereditary lockstep of dreams and hopes, and his quest becomes that of Henrik Ibsen's Oswald Alving or of Dr. Johnson's Rasselas—the "choice of life." His disappointment is with his own inability to become what he once thought of becoming. To this extent he derives more from the scientific rationalism of the eighteenth century than from the Augustinianism of the seventeenth. What is missing from all these efforts to achieve the "choice of life" is the ecstatic joy of having once succeeded.

Tracing these failures are the four poems which close the book, "Memories of West Street and Lepke," "Man and Wife," " 'To Speak of Woe That Is in Marriage,' " and "Skunk Hour." "Memories of West Street and Lepke" takes Lowell from his house on Marlborough Street out of the "tranquillized *Fifties*" back to his "fire-breathing" days as a Roman Catholic and his confinement as a conscientious objector in 1944. Like his father's haunting of the Maritime Museum in Salem, it represents a return to the time when Lowell had hopes and dreams and the ambition to realize them. Throughout this reverie crop up the forces of conformity, putting the world into a place "where even the man / scavenging filth in the back alley trash cans, / has two children, a beach wagon, a helpmate, / and is a 'young Republican.' "

For Lowell and the marijuana-smoking Negro of the poem, the force is imprisonment; for Abramowitz, the already imprisoned pacifist and vegetarian, it is the fists of "Bioff and Brown, / the Hollywood pimps." For the Jehovah's Witness, it is the stultifying routine of the "hospital tuck," and finally, when all else fails to achieve its end, it is the figure of Czar Lepke:

> *Flabby, bald, lobotomized,*
> *he drifted in a sheepish calm,*
> *where no agonizing reappraisal*
> *jarred his concentration on the electric chair—*
> *hanging like an oasis in his air*
> *of lost connections....*

This "sheepish" figure of Lepke turns on the earlier figures of Lowell and Lowell's father, recalling Lowell's own sense of being lobotomized and tranquilized and the Commander's loss of hope.

The electric chair, as a force of punishment and confinement, turns to electric-shock therapy and relates to the marijuana in the Negro's hair. Thus, society catches the individual in a network of conformity. Rather than bringing spiritual damnation, the result brings loss of identity and the destruction of the individual's hopes and dreams. Throughout the poem Lowell's "fire-breathing" Catholicism echoes his father's vain pursuits of "Anchors Aweigh" and *Glimpses of Unfamiliar Japan,* both to be lost somehow in being's eventual compromises with reality.

The voice is mature, and the technique, like the techniques of the three poems which follow, is a compromise between Lowell's earlier emphasis on events and his new time shift. Pattern, not the sequence of events, is important, but the events are arranged more sequentially than in "My Last Afternoon with Uncle Devereux Winslow."

Made to conform and further "tamed by *Miltown,*" the figures in the poems "Man and Wife" and " 'To Speak of Woe That Is in Marriage' " image tradition as a second means of stultification. Lying with his wife on his mother's "big-as-a-bathroom" bed in "Man and Wife," the poet recalls the evening they first met at a party given by Philip Rahv, editor of the *Partisan Review.* There, in her twenties, she had let go an invective against tradition which had "scorched the traditional South." Twelve years later, "the old-fashioned tirade— / loving, rapid, merciless— / breaks like the Atlantic Ocean" on his head.

Tradition, which prompts his failure and which had been the means his mother used to force his father out of the Navy into the failures of a social life, becomes for him a second means of control. Applied to the tirade, the Atlantic, which has always been a releasing force in Lowell's poetry, indicates the direction his life should be taking—away from tradition; yet the magnolia and the house, and the security and direction they offer prey upon the poet's own sense of insecurity and indirection and reassure him of his "sane" grasp of reality.

" 'To Speak of Woe That Is in Marriage' " speaks of the conflicts in the wife whose husband's sanity is fragmentary. Inscribed with a spliced quotation from Arthur Schopenhauer's *The World as Will and Idea* ("It is the future generation that presses into being by means of these exuberant feelings and supersensible soap bubbles of ours"), the poem investigates the traditions on which mar-

riage is continued as Ibsen's *Ghosts* had done two generations before. There, as Mrs. Alving had put up with the profligacy of her
husband for the sake of tradition, only to have her son suffer, now
the wife is putting up with the profligacy and insanity of her husband. The suffering of the poem is her own, and, torn by the traditions of the magnolia blossoms, she puts up with it. Yet behind
the suffering, the poem seems to ask under what conditions is a
woman justified in walking out; as Ibsen did, Lowell leaves the
ultimate answer to the conscience of his audience.

The last poem of the volume, "Skunk Hour," deals further
with these problems of tradition and conformity and portrays summer life on Nautilis Island. Outlining the major inhabitants of the
resort, from the "hermit heiress" to the "fairy decorator," Lowell
moves to a consideration of his own perverse experiences there,
searching for moonlight lovers parked along the highways. Alone,
in the religious despair of St. John of the Cross's "one dark night,"
listening to the radios "bleat" "O Careless Love," the poet realizes
his "mind's not right." He becomes the melancholy, suicidal Josiah
Hawley of "After the Surprising Conversions": "as though some
peddler groaned / . . . . 'My friend, / Cut your own throat. Cut
your own throat." He is John Milton's Lucifer in Book IV of
Paradise Lost: "I myself am hell." Finally, he comes across some
skunks, searching in the moonlight for a bite to eat. Food, their sub-
sistence, is thus equated with love, the motivation of his being
there. Experimenting, he tries to scare them off but they will not
scare. He is too like them or too insignificant to generate a sense of
fear. Yet in the skunks he sees some reason for going on. As he describes the progress of the poem in *The Contemporary Poet as
Artist and Critic* (Boston, 1964): "My night is not gracious, but
secular, puritan, and agnostical. An Existentialist night. Somewhere
in my mind was a passage from Sartre or Camus about reaching
some point of final darkness where the one free act is suicide. Out
of this comes the march and affirmation, an ambiguous one, of my
skunks in the last two stanzas."

In each of these poems, the poet through self-effacement tries
to arouse a sense of understanding and forgiveness. Man at his low-
est is too pitiable, too like the skunks, to be respected or held in
awe; yet there is something in him, an animal commitment to life,
which thwarts complete scepticism. Thus, the poems of "Life Studies" provide more than a new view of man's state; through public

confession, they are an attempt at purgation of the guilts which have built up over the course of a lifetime. Through this purgation, stripped to mere animal conviction, man may again build a system of values. In this particular case, the guilts they describe derive from Lowell's failure to live up to his grandfather's hopes, his mother's undermining of her husband's hopes, and his own mismanagement of things. His skill as a poet saves their expression from being maudlin and embarrassingly personal, for artistically the poems do succeed.

The time shift has succeeded in getting rid of the last vestiges of Joycean epicism, plot, and with this elimination the characters have become more human. In doing so, the poems no longer demand heroes reminiscent of great heroes of the past, for the age of accomplishment belongs only to those "who once thought the world their egg-shell." In them, man has become a thing, a sheep in the world's vast sheep pen, losing whatever he had that sought God's likeness and enlisting only comparisons with soulless animals. Consequently, in shedding plot and heroism, the poems have begun to err in an extreme opposite to the view that once demanded that everyone become a mystic. Rather than being "fractiously vindictive," the poems have become religiously despairing. They image the world as made up of compromise and failure and man as unable to achieve his dreams or be satisfied with less.

In this view of *Life Studies* is the final understanding of the inarticulate man who tries to live well but who cannot function on the intellectual or the religious level of awareness. In it, also, are excuses for the more articulate ones. Somewhere, Christianity with its emphasis on salvation has left, and humanity with its worldly accomplishments has come in. But there are dangers in this view and Stephen Spender points them out: "It ["Commander Lowell"] is a brilliant characterization but perhaps a bit too final. This finality is the strength of the poetry, but also constitutes a danger for it. . . . The danger is that the essence of an invisible world which is poetry will be excluded."

The poet who emerged in 1944 as "consciously a Catholic poet" can no longer find souls to be saved. What had been Lowell's religious view has turned into a soulless world of conformity. In the process, Conrad Aiken's hopes that Lowell might "expand his range" and try things of a "non-religious sort" have been fulfilled. R. P. Blackmur's objections to the "fractious vindictiveness" and the "nearly blasphemous" nature of the character portrayals have been resolved by their removal from his writing. However, man caught in the network of society is treated as vindictively as he was when caught in the lockstep of time. The later one is as materially destroyed as the other was spiritually. Nevertheless, in an age which likes to separate its religion from its art, the technical accomplishments of *Life Studies* may far outweigh the loss of the Christian experience. Most reviewers thought so when the book appeared. Elizabeth Bishop, an important American poet, wrote of its accomplishments: "Somehow or other, by fair means or foul, and in the middle of our worst century so far, we have produced a magnificent poet."

CHAPTER NINE

For the Union Dead

For the Union Dead (1964) continues the conceptual break with the image of man Lowell formed with such metaphysical certainty in his early volumes. Its thesis, a further expansion of sentiments which earlier introduced the noncontemplative pursuits of plot and character, constitutes a reversal of centers of importance and marks the triumph of "mere secularization and a craving for mechanical order" which had long been part of his vision. Formerly, grace made the soul the active force in the universe, but now the universe acts upon man, and what had been a religious concern for man's soul becomes a psychological concern for his mind. Thus, man, like the Cain figure of *Land of Unlikeness*, is robbed of his free will, and his feeble attempts at right choice are spiritually meaningless. This works to reshape Lowell's style which here moves away from a willed poetry to a poetry of impressions. As such, the volume both opposes and expands the view of man outlined in the final pages of *Life Studies*. When, in "Skunk Hour," deprived of love, stripped to mere animal conviction, and having come through the soul's dark night and a decision not to commit suicide, man tried anew to build a system of values. Then he was left "hanging on a question mark," Lowell remarks, not knowing whether it was "a death rope or a lifeline." Destroyed by the last vestiges of moral will, he was unable to will moral action. Now there is no action—good or bad—merely responses.

Lowell prepares for this reversal in *Imitations* (1961), a collection of translations from the works of other poets. These translations, in essence, form the permanent products of past forms of the state against which, according to Ezra Pound, modern society must be judged. In doing so, they embrace a theory of history which more completely accepts the Heraclitean cyclicism suggested in Lowell's own work. They incorporate Heraclitus' views that knowledge is based upon perception by the senses and that everything is in an eternal flux. Nothing, therefore, can escape final destruction. The immediate result is to make *Imitations* greatly resemble Ovid's *Metamorphoses,* an attempt in classical times to incorporate Heraclitus' theory of history into literary form. Francis Parker's title-page drawing of a woman being changed into a tree emphasizes this resemblance. And as Ovid incorporated his fables—mainly translations—into a sequence of contrasts and repetitions involving many personalities, Lowell explains in the Introduction to his book that it, too, "is partly self-sufficient and separate from its sources, and should be first read as a sequence, one voice running through many personalities, contrasts, and repetitions." Moreover, inherent in both books is the moral decay of Ovid's world view. In Lowell the decay is reflected by the continued use of animal images. Thus, by way of "imitation" from Homer to Boris Pasternak—many of which do not follow their originals—Lowell gives voice to his own cosmic pessimism. He pictures one age after another in which civilizations and men are destroyed by hate, anger, love, war, hope, dreams, nature, and time. In all these ages, despite moments of reconstruction, man's will is powerless against the process. As he explains in "Sic Transit," final decay is inevitable, and the attempts of succeeding generations to forestall it by patching ancestral houses only permit the rot to "ooze away the frames and underpinnings."

But where this decay in Heraclitus ultimately reduces itself to fire, in *For the Union Dead* it reduces itself to imagination. To illustrate the reduction Lowell adds elements which were not a part of the image patterns of *Life Studies.* First, he adds a symbol of the imagination either as a bursting soap bubble, derived from Schopenhauer, Hawthorne, and Sir Francis Bacon, or as a turtle carrying the world on its back, derived from oriental mythology and psychologist Carl Jung. Next, he merges the Heraclitean cycles with the circles of Dante's Inferno, conveying as William Stafford indicates in the Chicago *Tribune,* a "gift for finding terror and stultification everywhere. He can sweep his programmed attention thru any air and pick up signals that will elegantly terrorize the reader." Finally, in this Inferno, he revokes Emerson's famous distinction of "two laws discrete"—"Law for man, and a law for thing." Man becomes truly animalistic, and the whole universe—man, animal, and thing—moves relentlessly to the same principle.

Thus, in the historical poems of the volume, Lowell combines the elements of this new view of man and Heraclitean cyclicism with the literary devices of direct interior monologue and free association to convey much of what is new in his poetry. In "Florence," for example, which summarizes the cyclicism and moral decay of *Imitations*, without Lowell's new stress on imagination, something prompts the speaker to long for modern Florence, remembered as black ink, cuttlefish, April, Communists, brothels, British fairies, and an illness which forced him to think. There, he concludes, the apple of wisdom was more human—more like man and more adapted to man. It took a long time to mellow. Even the horseshoe crabs with their swordgrass blackbone tails (recalling both the black ink and cuttlefish) seem made for children to grab and "throw strangling ashore."

The town becomes this image as the speaker remembers that it kills its tyrants as its children kill crabs. He recalls the cruel tower of Palazzo Vecchio as Mary McCarthy pictures it in *The Stones of Florence* (New York, 1959), "piercing the sky like a stone hypodermic needle." He imagines the Piazza della Signoria below, Donatello's statue of "Judith and Holofernes," Judith cutting off the tyrant's head, Cellini's "Perseus and Medusa" commissioned to celebrate a restored despotism, and a copy of Michelangelo's "David." They convey a tradition of children rising "sword in hand" to emulate the "hypodermic needle of the Palazzo" and to oppose the unheroic children's seizing the blackbone tails of the crabs. The speaker asks pity for the monsters who have been destroyed, leaving no more Judiths and Davids. His heart bleeds black blood (again recalling the black ink) for these creatures, especially the Gorgon, whose severed head swings in his memory like the lantern of Diogenes searching out true men. The association leaves the unstated conclusion that without monsters there can be no true men.

Following the same techniques of direct interior monologue and free association, the other historical poems complete the change. "Tenth Muse" emphasizes the imagination by adding a new, destructive Muse, Sloth, to the traditional nine sisters, thereby making even the inhabitants of heaven subject to the laws of creation, rot, and renewal. In "July in Washington," the circles of Dante's Inferno blend with those in Major Pierre Charles l'Enfant's original plan of the city to describe the seat of American government as a place in which the narrator yearns for purgatorial mountains "powdered blue as a girl's eyelid." "Buenos Aires" takes its reader to Argentina, where the final lines of "Inauguration Day: January 1953" are repeated in the mausoleums and "literal commemorative busts" of South American soldier bureaucrats. Here man is equated with animals, and the sentiment is repeated in "Law," where disparate but equalizing experiences are traded off in a parallel of lawlessness drawn between man and nature. As the natural inclinations of the narrator violate the laws of man by "bass-plugging on posted reservoirs," a man-made Norman canal violates the natural green lawn. In all these poems the recollections are portrayed as separate and fragmented experiences, linked by free association and underlying recurrent themes to the time-shift techniques of *Life Studies*.

The result of both these innovations and continuations on a practical level is the creation of two new prototypes devoid of religious imagination. For at least half of the volume, the major figure is a passive anomic extension of the figure in "Skunk Hour." He is solitary, loveless, helpless, and still "too like the skunks to be held in awe." In these characteristics he is very much like the figure of man described by Saul Bellow in *Recent American Fiction* (Washington, 1963): "Laboring to maintain himself, or perhaps an idea of himself (not always a clear idea), he feels the pressure of a vast public life, which may dwarf him as an individual while permitting him to be a giant in hatred or fantasy. In these circumstances he grieves, he complains, rages, or laughs. All the while he is aware of his lack of power, his inadequacy as a moralist, the nauseous pressure of the mass media and the weight of money and organization, of cold war and racial brutalities." The effect of this laboring and its resultant, destructive collapsing human relationships is to present in the volume a sense of paralyzing personal anguish. People react independent of historical processes, and values remain temporary, individual, and insignificant; and any social importance which they might suggest remains contingent on poetic contexts which defy comparisons with past forms of the state.

Images continually pair off and cancel out, and the consequent response, like that of a chess game, lies quite often in the brilliance and subtlety of the neutralizing moves.

Also in his self-concern and his abandonment of action for a life of isolation and alienation, the figure is very much like the Narcissus figure described by Sir Francis Bacon in *The Wisdom of the Ancients* (1609) and used by Allen Tate in his "Ode to the Confederate Dead," to which the title poem of the volume invites comparison: "This fable seems to paint the behavior and fortune of those, who, for their beauty, or other endowments, wherein nature (without any industry of their own) has graced and adorned them, are extravagantly fond of themselves: for men of such a disposition generally affect retirement, and absence from public affairs; as a life of business must necessarily subject them to many neglects and contempts, which might disturb or ruffle their minds: whence such persons commonly lead a solitary, private, and shadowy life: see little company, and those only such as highly admire and reverence them; or, like an echo, assent to all they say."

Resurrecting the figure for his poem, Tate comments in "Narcissus as Narcissus" (1938) that the Ode concerns "the cut-off-ness of the modern 'intellectual man' from the world." As such, it is concerned with "solipsism or Narcissism, or any other *ism* that denotes the failure of the human personality to function properly in nature and society." He explains that the terms "Narcissism" and "solipsism" are used "to mean only preoccupation with self; it may be love or hate." In the poem, Narcissism has led the figure to ask if he should worship death. On this question Tate writes: "The question is not answered, although as a kind of romanticism it might, if answered affirmatively, provide an illusory solution to the solipsism of the man; but he cannot accept it. Nor has he been able to live in his immediate world, the fragmentary cosmos. There is no practical solution. ... The main intention of the poem has been to state the conflict ... as experienced form—not as a logical dilemma." In "The Mills of the Kavanaughs" and "The Banker's Daughter," Lowell's heroines had already answered the question affirmatively, and the animal commitment to life in "Skunk Hour" is in effect a reversal of their answers.

This solipsistic figure receives fullest public treatment in the title poem of the volume. Relying heavily on borrowings from history, literature, and immediate experience, Lowell opposes the free associations of the figure's mind with fixed, outside objects in a general canceling out, time-shift structure. The result is a stasis in which the good intentions of the figure are negated by his inability to act. From history, Lowell appropriates the Shaw Memorial by Augustus St. Gaudens, which William James wished "to stand here for all time, an inciter to similarly unselfish public deeds." From the monument he derives the poem's inscription, a modification of the inscription composed by Harvard President Charles W. Eliot— "omnia relinquit servare rem publicam" ("he leaves all to serve the state"). The motto prepares one for the ironic ending in which not service but "servility slides by on grease."

From literature Lowell borrows the pattern of Tate's "Ode to the Confederate Dead." The opening description of the old South Boston Aquarium standing in a snow storm, its windows broken and its tanks dry, resembles the one of the dry leaves "rumor of mortality" which opens Tate's poem. His figure paused for a baroque meditation on the ravages of time, concluding with a figure of a blind crab. This creature, Tate explains, has mobility but no direction, energy but no purposeful world to use it in. "He is one of two explicit symbols for the locked-in ego, representing the cut-off-ness of the modern 'intellectual man' from the world." In Lowell, the description sets off a similar recollection in the speaker's mind of a time when his nose "tingled to burst the bubbles" of a fish tank. In this recollection, the metaphor of a snail becomes his own locked-in ego. The deserted aquarium reminds him of his still strong yearnings "for the dark downward and vegetating kingdom of fish and reptiles," suggestive of history from the Paleozoic to the Cenozoic ages. He recalls "one morning last March," pressing his nose against another screen behind which "yellow dinosaur steamshovels," reflective of these yearnings, "gouge" an underworld garage. He concludes that modern Boston has become a series of sandpiles for future garages and superhighways.

His eyes shift to the Shaw Monument which faces the State-house excavation. Like the Confederate dead of Tate's poem, Colonel Robert Shaw represents tradition. In life he led the 54th Massachusetts Infantry, the first colored regiment, nearly half of whose men were killed within or before the walls of Fort Wagner. According to William James, whose speech at the monument's unveiling provides some of the poem's detail, Shaw bore witness to the brotherhood of man: "As for the colonel,... his body, half stripped of its clothing, and the corpses of his dauntless negroes were flung into one common trench together, and the sand was shovelled over them, without a stake or stone to signalize the spot. In death as in life, then, the Fifty-fourth bore witness to the brotherhood of man. The lover of heroic history could wish for no more fitting sepulchre for Shaw's magnanimous young heart."

From the speech, Lowell not only borrows the comment that James "could almost hear the bronze Negroes breathe," but the sentiments that this monument reared "long after the abstract soldier's-monuments . . . on every village green" is "the first soldier's-monument to be raised to a particular set of comparatively undistinguished men." Also from a letter to Henry James, Lowell seems to borrow James's interest in the faces of his audience: "The thing that struck me most in the day was the faces of the old 54th soldiers, . . . such respectable old darkey faces, the heavy animal look entirely absent, and in its place the wrinkled, patient, good old darkey citizens." These faces become "the drained faces of Negro children rising like balloons" behind a television screen.

In the speech James indicates that he prefers the humanity of peace to the cruel heroism of war and cites two enemies which may be fought to the limit: physical nature and whatever opposes moral will. As time collapses and the ditch, suggestive of the "great ash-pit of Jehoshaphat" and the pit of hell, draws nearer, these enemies still must be defeated. There are no statues, the speaker notes, for what he infers is an unjustified, commercial last war. "On Boyleston Street, a commercial photograph / shows Hiroshima boiling / over a Mosler Safe, the 'Rock of Ages' / that survived the blast."

Space is the new frontier, but the brotherhood of man remains the immediate question posed by the Negroes in a school integration struggle. Resembling the situations of the aquarium and the garage this question remains behind a screen, and the speaker, like the figure of the Tate poem, is unable again to act or "function properly in nature and society." His isolation in the face of destruction sends Colonel Shaw, riding his bubble of the world, to world end. The aquarium disappears, and the signs of the new age—"grand finned cars nosing forward like fish"—evoke a new Paleozoic Age, where "a savage servility slides by on grease." Thus, the tensions of the poem remain identical with those of Tate's poem except for Lowell's own voice and two new elements: Within the opposition of man and tradition, a manufactured and

impersonal nature adds to the mortality of Tate's setting. In addition, the obvious backdrop of Heraclitean cyclicism precludes
man's ability to act in any way that might reverse the process.

On a less public level, the figure appears in "Water" and
"The Old Flame." The titles suggest purification and liberation,
whereas the texts deny such considerations. Set in Maine, the
poems concern the failures of love in Lowell's first, unsuccessful, eight-year marriage to Jean Stafford. In doing so, they
continue both his current device of free association and his
uses of landscape to interpret these associations. Of the first, John
Wain writes in "The New Robert Lowell" (1964): "The poem is
'about' a relationship, . . . which is haunted by tension and insecurity and ultimately breaks up. The pounding of the sea on the
rock, and the pathetic dream of the mermaid clinging to the pier
and trying to get rid of the hard, skin-tearing barnacles, even perhaps the emptiness of oyster shells which the bleak human habita-
tions bring to mind, all add up to a complete metaphor of this relationship and his failure, till the stabbing pathos of the last stanza"
—in which the figures of the poem find the water too cold to brave
and thereby reject the means offered them for purification—
"brings the poem ending, as cold and salt as Atlantic water."

The failure of this relationship and the isolation of experiences
from one another are manifested in both the opposing images of rock
and sea, past and present, fish and human, and the isolation of each
set of opposing images from the others. Within this separation,
people bob between mainland and quarry, the fish bob within the
mazes of a weir, and the mermaid clings to her wharf pile. As the
fish become bait for larger catches, all become sacrifices to larger
objectives, ending in a mutually destructive way of life. These
sacrifices—as the final separateness indicates—are rejected by the
poem's figures, and the element of this rejection forms the new
basis of failure.

"The Old Flame" records the moods set off by seeing the
house in Damariscotta, Maine, which inspired the setting for Miss
Stafford's "A Country Love Story" and sections of his "The Mills
of the Kavanaughs." The restoration which they planned once but
never executed has been carried out by others in a way they
rejected. The house resembles Henry Ford's restoration of the
Wayside Inn. Indian maize is on the door, a flag on a flagpole, and
the clapboards are painted a schoolhouse red. A new landlord, a

new wife, a new hope have effected these changes. Even the whole "new frontier" of a Kennedy administration has occurred since the events prompting these works.

He envisions the imaginary lover of the story "staring through the window," where his apparition "tightens" a scarf about his throat, introducing a suicidal element not in the original, in which both husband and wife exacted avenging lovers out of their solitudes. He toasts the new people and comments that everything "has been swept clean" and "changed for the best" since they lived there "in one bed and apart," hearing what in the story Miss Stafford calls "the ditcher on snowy nights rising with a groan over the hill, flinging the snow from the road and warning of its approach by lights that first flashed red, then blue." Again the fusing and cleansing force of fire suggested by the poem's title has failed. There have been no mergings, no bendings of will.

In all three poems it becomes apparent that what prompts the isolation and comprises the "beauty" or "other endowment" which turns man into a Narcissus figure is "sensibility." This echoes Bellow's statement that "what the young American writer most often appears to feel is his own misfortune. The injustice is done to his talent if life is brutish and ignorant, if the world seems overcome by spam and beer, or covered with detergent lathers and poisonous monoxides. This apparently is the only injustice he feels. Neither for himself nor for his fellows does he attack power and injustice directly and hotly. He simply defends his sensibility." It is made even more explicit in the compulsive and brutish outside world described in "The Mouth of the Hudson," "Fall 1961," "Eye and Tooth," "Going to and fro," and "Myopia: a Night." In these, faint echoes of the old Christian experience sound. They are heard in the returning image of time as the ticking of a clock, ticking away, like judgments of man, the significances of his accomplishments, and in the normal, natural rot which repeats these judgments. They are present, too, in a recurrent spider image that merges Jonathan Edwards' comparison of depraved man in "Mr. Edwards and the Spider" with Sir Francis Bacon's attack on man's attempts to tie the fragments of his experiences together by means of abstract philosophy in *The Advancement of Learning:* "But if it [the wit and mind of man] work upon itself, as the spider worketh his web, then it is endless, and brings forth indeed cobwebs of learning, admirable for the fineness of thread and work, but of no substance or profit." Behind these returns is a judgment of man which sees abstract and scientific knowledge equally culpable in producing hubris and massive destruction, yet views the effects mainly in material terms. Although there are indications of a Faust figure, there is no merging grace of a St. Bernard prototype. When the figure succeeds in getting out of himself, as he does in "New York 1962: Fragment," it is only to reverse the image in "The Old Flame," in which husband and wife slept "in one bed and apart." Afterward, despite the poem's esctasy, it closes walls about its lovers and sets a "wooden workhorse working here below." The world about remains hostile.

In the second half of the volume, after the prolonged brooding upon past and current wrongs, an epical version of this figure emerges. The narrator becomes less interested in personal responses and begins to view them as derivative of conditions where the center of emotional gravity has become as removed from him as it is from others. In this shift the poems move out of the pre-speech level of consciousness and free association into older established forms. "The Public Garden," a recasting of "David and Bathsheba in the Public Garden," for example, restores the dramatic monologue devices of *The Mills of the Kavanaughs*. This restoration, incorporating the new stresses on sensibility and imagination, makes apparent the new ideal figure which replaces the once exemplary epical figure of St. Bernard. It is the figure of the writer. Moreover, as this epical figure once corrected his nature in anticipation of the mystical experience, the writer now corrects his nature in anticipation of the imaginative experience. This experience, an escape from the Heraclitean cyclicism of the world by uniting with the world's first principle of imagination, approximates the earlier religious escapes from the damning lockstep of time, but like the psychical escapes of *Life Studies*, it remains independent of salvation.

"Hawthorne" and "Jonathan Edwards in Western Massachusetts" most fully develop the features of this figure, his correction, and his escape. In doing so they combine the structure of the character sketches in *Life Studies*, in which Lowell first dealt with artistic immortality along mystical lines, with the contemplative poems of *Land of Unlikeness* and *Lord Weary's Castle*. From *Life Studies* he appropriates the function of the writer to illumine history, not the divine, and the sacrifices which his nature, the nature of his craft, and a hostile society force upon him. But instead of

personal illuminations, these sacrifices now end in worldly illuminations consistent with Lowell's sweeping, morally determined view
of history. From the contemplative poems, Lowell derives the pattern of these illuminations by making the sacrifices correspond to
the prayers and self-examination of the contemplative prior to his
mystical encounters.

Thus, "Hawthorne," written for the Centenary Edition of
Hawthorne's works, shows evidences of both structures as it deline-
ates the figure. Like the character sketches of *Life Studies*, it uses
phrases from Hawthorne's writings. The opening description of
Salem comes from "The Custom House" introduction to *The Scarlet Letter:* "This old town of Salem . . . its flat, unvaried surface,
covered with wooden houses, . . . its long and lazy street lounging
wearisomely through the whole extent of the peninsula, with Gal-
lows Hill and New Guinea at one end, and a view of the almshouse
at the other. . . ." The description depicts the hostile, sterile society in which the writer functions. From it, Lowell drifts to the
present, picking up an image of tarnished plate paralleling the
writer's limitations in Hawthorne's statement: "My imagination
was a tarnished mirror. It would not reflect, or only with miserable
dimness, the figures with which I did my best to people it."

Having laid out both the physical and mental landscape, the
poem drops to the figure of Hawthorne humbly and monkishly
"measuring out coal and mostly trying to keep warm." Then it
drifts to a black schooner, the South-end dock, a steeple with a
clock, all constricting symbols of decay, and returns to show Hawthorne, now "walking on top of the blazing roof" and "feeling
those flashes that char the discharged cells of the brain." These
flashes, suggestive of ecstasy as well as the purposeful bubbles of the
imagination, recall the final picture of George Santayana in *Life
Studies*. Their importance is immediately emphasized by a comparison of Hawthorne's face with the faces of his contemporaries,
Longfellow, Lowell, Holmes, and Whittier. They are described as
"frizzled," recalling the "frizzled lilacs" of the dead elders in "At
the Indian Killer's Grave" and the "frizzled" look of Lowell after
his shock treatments in "Home After Three Months Away." Hawthorne's face has a "blond mustache," a "golden General Custer
scalp," and a "survivor's smile."

No longer concerned with personal lessons, the poem concludes with a general statement that Hawthorne has achieved his

liberation and immortality by brooding upon the commonest things, by meditation on the true and insignificant. This brooding subsequently becomes the source of the new anagogic path of knowledge which the new epical figure must undertake. What this knowledge is, however, is left undefined as the poem ends like "The North Sea Undertaker's Complaint" and "Colloquy in Black Rock" at the moment of union. Neither the vision nor the active life induced by such a vision is depicted. But even then, this humanistic active life would prove spiritually meaningless without God's grace.

In the prospect of a Dantean Inferno, "Jonathan Edwards in Western Massachusetts" pictures Edwards' sacrifices to achieve self-knowledge. As with "Hawthorne," the emphasis is narcissistic. The poem, Lowell's third about Edwards, thereby contrasts with the earlier poems, where the intent was to use Edwards' writings to create primarily a character portrayal which would convey a moral message to the modern world. In both poems the message had to do with the conflict of merchant and religious interests which accordingly caused the breach between Edwards and his congregation and forced him out of Northampton. Hence, their concerns were primarily with the correction of others. Now the concern is self-correction. As such, the poem ends with Edwards' own summary of his nature: "First my own defects, unfitting me for such an undertaking, many of which are generally known; . . . I have a constitution, in many respects peculiarly unhappy, attended with flaccid solids; vapid, sizy and scarce fluids, and a low tide of spirits; often occasioning a kind of childish weakness and contemptibleness of speech, presence, and demeanor; with a disagreeable dulness and stiffness. . . ." This self-correction again does not constitute salvation, for as Lowell announces, he and Edwards "move in different circles," and the writer, regardless of his pretended escapes from the historical cyclicism about him, retains his position in the flux and remains morally depraved.

The poem opens with the statement that Edwards' "great millstone and rock of hope has crumbled," suggesting that his religious views have passed. Those he opposed—"the square white houses of his flock"—remain triumphant, but they are outside God's grace "like sheep outside the fold." Man has learned to live in doubt, to "do without faith." Thus, in the hostility between the writer and society, Edwards' misconception of world end opposes modern conceptions of world end as man grows daily farther from the Pilgrim reminiscences of England, the Promised Land, and paradise. In this opposition, memories of England, based in the main on readings of Sir Francis Bacon, enter Edwards' mind. Whitehall, the Royal Palace, becomes the metaphor for any country house imbued with the presence of God. Gardens, utilizing phrases from Bacon's essay "Of Gardens," merge with the gardens of Edwards' "Personal Narrative," where holiness makes "the soul like a field or a garden of God, with all manner of pleasant flowers." These spiritual gardens, like York House which Bacon refused to sell on his fall from power, in the next stanza become something which Edwards, too, refuses to sell in order to remain in Northampton. Language and metaphor of this refusal derive from the essay "Of Vaine-Glory," in which Bacon speaks of his learning as "feathers." The hostility of society is then summed up in the humoring phrase, "Ah, Paradise!" as the narrator goes on to say that he would be afraid of Edwards' rigorous paradise and that they ultimately travel in different circles, not only of time, but of thought and damnation. The persecution of Edwards thus resembles the persecution of the Cistercians in "Cistercians in Germany."

The poem shifts to the sacrifices of Edwards' nature, based on biographical information. It opens with a mixture of Edwards' essays "Of Insects," "Personal Narrative," and "Sarah Pierrepont." From "Personal Narrative" it takes the episode of Edwards' building "a booth in a swamp, in a very retired spot, for a place of prayer." From "Sarah Pierrepont," it uses the description of his wife: "They say there is a young lady who is beloved of that Great Being, who . . . comes to her and fills her mind with exceeding sweet delight, and that she hardly cares for anything. . . . She will sometimes go about from place to place, singing sweetly, and . . . loves to be alone, walking in the fields and groves, and seems to have some one invisible always conversing with her." It continues with an almost direct quotation from Edwards' "Sinners in the Hand of an Angry God" and ends with an observation from Sir Francis Bacon's "Of Great Places": "All rising is by a winding stair."

After this illumination, the poem returns the reader to modern Northampton which, as a relic of Edwards, has merely a slice of an oak tree he is said to have planted. As a piece of wood fit only for burning, the relic recalls the thorns of Isaiah (33:12) which shall "be burnt in the fire," and having once been green, the statement in Job (14:7) that "A tree hath hope: if it be cut, it groweth green again, and the boughs thereof sprout." Edwards' convictions, however, at Northampton became "all black and white," like the somber sky descending over Boston in "Where the Rainbow Ends." They have none of the gray of doubt.

The narrator explains that he prefers the faded, old, exiled figure who was afraid to leave Stockbridge and his last congregation, a group of Housatonic Indian children, and his writing, writing, writing, which in "Freedom of the Will" denied Free Will. In that treatise Edwards argued that all acts of will, like events in physical nature, are subject to the laws of causation and finally that the will has no independent activity but is merely passive and mechanical. The idea, embraced already in Lowell's new view of man, reduces man, animal, and thing, to the same law of will. The poem then concludes with the already quoted description of Edwards to the Board of Trustees of the College of New Jersey (now Princeton) commenting on his qualifications to assume the office of president.

The natures of the volume's lyrical and epical prototypes suggest the sensibilities which produced the lyrical poems of *Life Studies* and the epical and dramatic poems of the previous volumes, with one exception. Unlike Lowell, these sensibilities are unaware of the "memory of the spiritual dignity of man" which underlies the Heraclitean cyclicism and their lack of will. Otherwise, they function to define a self, not in dramatic external actions, but in a private vision of reality—what life subjectively is—to correspond to already depicted external figures. In doing so, they complete on a different level of awareness the self-examination begun in *Life Studies*. Consequently, they continue to approximate the efforts of W. B. Yeats's middle period when, through recollection, the basis for his later, elaborate personal mythology was established. In this approximation, the poems rely on the current intellectual emphases on psychological motive and deemphasis on action to stress, as the basis of common experience, the psychological motives and moods which many sensitive Americans share rather than any action which might be construed as important in the formation of a nation or race. In addition, they seek to make the sensibility of the writer, and consequently of Lowell, important by restoring the romantic importance and function of writing. In this attempt, they echo Matthew Arnold's well-known statement on the destiny of poetry:

> The future of poetry is immense, because in poetry, where it is worthy of its high destinies, our race, as time goes on, will find an ever surer and surer stay. There is not a creed which is not shaken, not an accredited dogma which is not shown to be questionable, not a received tradition which does not threaten to dissolve. Our religion has materialized itself in the fact, in the supposed fact; it has attached its emotion to the fact, and now the fact is failing it. But for poetry the idea is everything; the rest is a world of illusion, of divine illusion. Poetry attaches its emotion to the idea; the idea *is* the fact. The strongest part of our religion to-day is its unconscious poetry.

In the lyrical poems of the volume, where the prototype is an extension of the author and the subject matter "the simplest verbal vesture of an instant emotion," the discrepancy between Lowell and the persona is least noticeable. Here Lowell weds beautifully the cadences of a personal voice with personal experiences into a poetry reflective of self-knowledge and human failures. He accomplishes what Babette Deutsch in "The Teacher" (1959) describes as the two essentials of "technical excellence"—economy, the absence of the superfluous but not necessarily of ornament, and accuracy, the achievement of appropriate cadences and words. Still, as the awarding of the Bollingen Prize to Ezra Pound suggested in 1949 and the reviews of *Life Studies* continued ten years later, there is a judgment of an art work which sees it in terms of content as well as form and insists that the meaning of poetry is as important as its cadences.

The disagreements of reviewers over this content have not been helped by the nonlyrical poems, in which the separation of Lowell from the poems' personae becomes more marked. Here his awareness of historical processes clashes with his fixing of responsibility, and a situation develops similar to that in *The Mills of the Kavanaughs* when Lowell tried to fit everyone to a contemplative mold. As the meditational approach then worked against his non-meditational subject matter, his Christianized Heraclitean cyclicism now works against his poet-Christian man. The effect is to recall

R. P. Blackmur's objections to *Land of Unlikeness* (1945): "It is as if he [Lowell] demanded *to know* (to judge, to master) both the substance apart from the form with which he handles it and the form apart from the substance handled in order to set them fighting." He is no closer to finding in verse what Blackmur calls "a tension of necessity," which has, when recognized, "the quality of conflict accepted." His work still "grits" instead of resolves, especially as it no longer contains both a view of corruption and a pattern of salvation; it has only the corruption.

The effect of this clash on the overall impression of the book and on Lowell's future as a poet is one of confusion. Lowell's failure to take advantage of the aesthetic distance offered him in order to form a workable attitude toward his prototypes results in no attitude at all. The nature, sources, and positions of the personae demand that they be viewed comically, tragically, or clinically, yet at moments when he should be detached Lowell continually slips into self-pity, and what begins as an attack on narcissism ends as an attack on the world. This attack comes no closer to solving the causes of narcissism than does the alienation. In addition, although both sensibilities are different from Lowell's, his insistence on defining them in terms of mind rather than as physical entities results in a picture of man as an amorphous, elusive "receiving device" which defies comprehension, even biographically. This is partly the fault of the derangement of values which results from a loss of grace, but it is also a fault of the volume's structure, for rather than merging the short poems into some impression organized to present a single sensibility, it permits the isolated and fragmented experiences described to become even more isolated and fragmented in an onslaught of disparate, chaotic reactions. Moreover, the subjective emphasis of the volume runs the same risk of most impressionistic literature as well as of Lowell's first published poem, "The Cities' Summer Death," namely that of vacillating between a private and public voice and ultimately perhaps of providing too little information for the reader.

Still, it would be unwise to ignore the accomplishments of *For the Union Dead* or Lowell's awareness of the book's shortcomings. The vision behind the poems is vast, and, when regarded apart from the Heraclitean determinism, many poems engage a reader's strong sympathies, attesting to the poetic skill present. Moreover, the volume's amorphous figures and emphasis on public life provide within the structure of historical determinism a workable basis for resolving the breach between form and substance, Lowell and his personae. There is evidence, too, of a possible abandoning of the historical view as earlier Lowell had abandoned his religious structures. "Caligula," for example, which draws a correspondence between Lowell's nickname "Cal" and the nickname of the Roman Emperor Gaius Caesar Augustus Germanicus, despite a debt to Suetonius' *Lives of the Caesars*, owes considerable to the apostle of the Absurd in Albert Camus' play, *Caligula*. Camus' Caligula discovered that there was no answer to the problem of suffering: "Men die and they are not happy." Imitating the cruel and senseless gods, he creates a momentary world whose qualities are the same as those of Lowell's narcissistic world—the relentless isolation of man, the equal unimportance of all actions, and justification through imagination. The presence of these two disparate possibilities in the volume precludes any quick, "rocklike" resolutions in Lowell's writing and suggests that his thinking resembles the imaginative process depicted in "Tenth Muse," by "beginning in wisdom and dying in doubt." The future and hope in this doubt, echoing the march and ambiguous Existential affirmation of the skunks in "Skunk Hour," may explain Lowell's optimism after the book's publication. Disregarding the noose image he used to describe his attitude on completing *Life Studies*, he said: "Thankfully, the lifeline seems to me both longer and stronger than I thought at that time."

Bibliography

Adams, Henry. *The Education of Henry Adams.* Boston, 1918.

Aiken, Conrad. "Varieties of Poetic Statement," *The New Republic,* CXI (1944), 528–30.

Bacon, Sir Francis. *Bacon's Essays and Wisdom of the Ancients.* Boston, 1899.

Bancroft, George. *Martin Van Buren.* New York, 1889.

Bellow, Saul. *Recent American Fiction.* Washington, 1963.

Bennett, Joseph. "Two Americans, a Brahmin and the Bourgeoisie," *Hudson Review,* XII (1959), 431–39.

Bernard, Saint. *On the Love of God,* tr. Terence L. Connolly. Westminster, Md., 1951.

———. *On the Song of Songs,* tr. a religious of C.S.M.V. London, 1952.

———. *The Steps of Humility,* ed. George Bosworth Burch. Cambridge, Mass., 1942.

Blackmur, R. P. "Notes on Eleven Poets," *Kenyon Review,* VII (1945), 339–52.

Bonaventure, Saint. *Meditations on the Life of Christ,* tr. Sr. M. Emmanuel, O.S.B. St. Louis, 1934.

Boulenger, Jacques. *The Seventeenth Century.* New York, [n.d.]

Butler, Alban. *The Lives of the Saints,* ed. and rev. Herbert Thurston, S.J., and Donald Attwater. 10 vols. London, 1934.

Cobbett, William. *Rural Rides,* ed. Pitt Cobbett. 2 vols. London, 1893.

Deutsch, Babette. "The Teacher." In William Van O'Connor and Edward Stone, *Casebook on Ezra Pound.* New York, 1959.

Edwards, Jonathan. *Jonathan Edwards,* ed. Clarence H. Faust and Thomas H. Johnson. New York, 1935.

———. *The Works of the Reverend Jonathan Edwards.* 8 vols. Worcester, 1808.

Eliot, T. S. *Selected Essays.* London, 1952.

Ford, Ford Madox. *It Was the Nightingale.* Philadelphia, 1933.

Frankenberg, Lloyd. *Pleasure Dome.* Boston, 1949.

Giovannini, Giovanni. "Lowell's 'After the Surprising Conversions,'" *The Explicator,* IX (June, 1951), 53.

Gordon, Caroline. "The Story of Ford Madox Ford," *Highlights of Modern Literature*, ed. Francis Brown. Mentor Books. New York, 1954.

✗ Gunn, Thom. "Excellences and Variety," *Yale Review*, XLIX (1960), 295–305.

Hawthorne, Nathaniel. *Mosses from an Old Manse*. Philadelphia, 1890.

——. *The Scarlet Letter*. Rinehart Books. New York, 1947.

Humphrey, Robert. *Stream of Consciousness in the Modern Novel*. Berkeley, Calif., 1958.

James, William. *The Letters of William James*, ed. Henry James, Jr. 2 vols. Boston, 1920.

——. *Memories and Studies*. New York, 1917.

Jarrell, Randall. *Poetry and the Age*. Vintage Books. New York, 1955.

Joyce, James. *The Portable James Joyce*, ed. Harry Levin. New York, 1949.

Jung, Carl G. *Contributions to Analytical Psychology*, tr. H. C. and C. F. Baynes. London, 1928.

Kenner, Hugh. *The Poetry of Ezra Pound*. London, 1951.

Kunitz, Stanley, "Talk with Robert Lowell," New York *Times Book Review*, October 4, 1964, pp. 34–38.

Lincoln, Charles H., ed. *Narratives of the Indian Wars: 1675–1699*. New York, 1952.

Lowell, Robert. "The Cities' Summer Death," *Kenyon Review*, I (1939), 32.

——. "Death from Cancer on Easter," *Sewanee Review*, LI (1943), 390.

——. *For the Union Dead*. New York, 1964.

——. *Imitations*. New York, 1961.

——. "An Interview," *Paris Review*, XXV (1961), 56–95.

——. *Land of Unlikeness*. Cummington, Mass., 1944.

——. *Life Studies*. New York, 1959.

——. *Lord Weary's Castle*. New York, 1946.

——. *The Mills of the Kavanaughs*. New York, 1951.

——. "The Muses Won't Help Twice," *Kenyon Review*, XVII (1955), 317–24.

——. "A Note," *Kenyon Review*, VI (1944), 583–86.

Bibliography

——. "On Robert Lowell's 'Skunk Hour,'" *The Contemporary Poet as Artist and Critic*, ed. Anthony Ostroff. Boston, 1964.

——. "The Poetry of John Berryman," *New York Review of Books*, II (May 28, 1964), 3–4.

——. "Prayer for the Jews," *Sewanee Review*, LI (1943), 395.

——. "Prose Genius in Verse," *Kenyon Review*, XV (1953), 619–25.

——. "A Review of T. S. Eliot's *Four Quartets*," *Sewanee Review*, LI (1943), 432–35.

——. "Santayana's Farewell to His Nurses," *Perspectives U.S.A.*, III (1953), 67.

——. "Thomas, Bishop and Williams," *Sewanee Review*, LV (1947), 493–504.

Lynch, William F. *Christ and Apollo*. Mentor-Omega Books. New York, 1963.

Mann, Thomas. *Stories of Three Decades*, tr. H. T. Lowe-Porter. New York, 1945.

McCarthy, Mary. "Settling the Colonel's Hash," *Harper's*, CCVIII (February, 1954), 68–75.

——. *The Stones of Florence*. New York, 1959.

Melville, Herman. *Moby Dick or The White Whale*. Rinehart Books. New York, 1950.

Mènasce, Jean C. de. "Leviathan Come to Pass," *The Commonweal*, XXXVII (1942–43), 64–68.

Nietzsche, Friedrich. *The Philosophy of Nietzsche*. New York, 1927.

Nims, John F. "Two Catholic Poets," *Poetry*, LXV (1944–45), 264–68.

Pearce, Roy Harvey. *The Continuity of American Poetry*. Princeton, 1961.

Pick, John. *Hopkins, Priest and Poet*. London, 1942.

Pound, Ezra. *Guide to Kulchur*. Norfolk, Conn., 1938.

Raleigh, Sir Walter. *The History of the World in Five Books*. London, 1687.

Sales, Saint Francis de. *Treatise on the Love of God*, tr. Rev. Henry Benedict Mackey, O.S.B. Westminster, Md., 1942.

Santayana, George. *Dominations and Powers*. New York, 1951.

——. *The Letters of George Santayana*, ed. Daniel Cory. New York, 1955.

Spender, Stephen. "Robert Lowell's Family Album," *The New Republic*, CXL (1959), 17.

Stafford, Jean. *Children Are Bored on Sunday*. New York, 1953.

Stafford, William. "Poems That Deal a Jolt," Chicago *Tribune Books Today*, November 15, 1964, p. 11.

Staples, Hugh B. *Robert Lowell: The First Twenty Years*. New York, 1962.

Tate, Allen. "Narcissus as Narcissus," *Virginia Quarterly Review*, XIV (1938), 108–22.

Thiébault, Baron. *The Memoirs of Baron Thiébault*, tr. Arthur J. Butler. London, 1896.

Wain, John. "The New Robert Lowell," *The New Republic*, CLI (October 17, 1964), 21–23.

Watkin, Edward I. *Catholic Art and Culture*. New York, 1944.

Watts, Harold H. *Ezra Pound and the Cantos*. London, 1953.

Werfel, Franz. *Poems*. Princeton, 1945.

Weston, Jessie L. *From Ritual to Romance*. Anchor Books. Garden City, N.Y., 1957.

White, Morton. *The Age of Analysis*. Mentor Books. New York, 1955.

Willey, Basil. *Eighteenth Century Background*. New York, 1946.

Index

Index

Index

143

Index